Virginia Foundation
1987

27 ^{95}

PROLOGUE

Recent Titles in
Contributions in American Studies
Series Editor: Robert H. Walker

PROLOGUE

The Novels of
Black American
Women,
1891–1965

CAROLE McALPINE WATSON

Contributions in American Studies, Number 79

GREENWOOD PRESS
WESTPORT, CONNECTICUT
LONDON, ENGLAND

Library of Congress Cataloging in Publication Data

Watson, Carole McAlpine.
 Prologue : the novels of Black American women,
1891–1965.

 (Contributions in American studies, ISSN 0084-9227; no. 79)
 Bibliography: p.
 Includes index.
 1. American fiction—Afro-American authors—History
and criticism.   2. Afro-Americans in literaure.
3. Afro-American women in literature.   4. American
fiction—Women authors—History and criticism.
5. American fiction—20th century—History and criticism.

I. Title. II. Series.
PS374.N4W37 1985   813'.009'9287   84-21265
ISBN 0-313-23630-5 (lib. bdg.)

Library of Congress Catalog Card Number: 84-21265
ISBN: 0-313-23630-5
ISSN: 0084-9227

First published in 1985

Greenwood Press
A division of Congressional Information Service, Inc.
88 Post Road West
Westport, Connecticut 06881

Printed in the United States of America

10 9 8 7 6 5 4 3 2 1

Copyright Acknowledgments

 For permission to use copyrighted material, I gratefully acknowledge the
following:
Excerpts from *Moses: Man of the Mountain* by Zora Neale Hurston. J. B. Lippincott Co. Copyright 1939 by Zora Neale Hurston; renewed 1967 by John C.
Hurston and Joel Hurston. Reprinted by permission of Harper & Row, Publishers, Inc., and J. M. Dent & Sons Ltd. Publisher.

Excerpts from *Jonah's Gourd Vine* by Zora Neale Hurston. J. B. Lippincott
Co. Copyright 1934 by Zora Neale Hurston; renewed 1962 by John Hurston.
Reprinted by permission of Harper & Row, Publishers, Inc., and by Gerald
Duckworth & Co. Ltd.

To my Parents
James Arnold and Carole Eunice McAlpine
To my children, Gregory and Dominic
And to Thomas Michael Keyes

First fight. Then fiddle. Ply the slipping string
With feathery socery; muzzle the note
With hurting love; the music that they wrote
Bewitch, bewilder. Qualify to sing
Threadwise. Devise no salt, no hempen thing
For the dear instrument to bear. Devote
The bow to silks and honey. Be remote
A while from malice and from murdering.
But first to arms, to armor. Carry hate
In front of you and harmony behind.
Be deaf to music and to beauty blind.
Win war. Rise bloody, maybe not too late
For having first to civilize a space
Wherein to play your violin with grace.

Gwendolyn Brooks Blakely, *The World of Gwendolyn Brooks*

CONTENTS

PREFACE

The cultural nationalism that characterized the civil rights struggle of black Americans during the 1960s affected numerous aspects of black American life. In the literary, visual, and performing arts, professional artists and thousands of amateurs produced works explicitly aimed at fostering the political and cultural survival of black people. Leading proponents of the Black Arts movement developed a race-centered theory of criticism, the Black Aesthetic, in which they defined new criteria for Afro-American art. Underlying the Black Aesthetic was an ethical position requiring that the creations of black artists be centered in the Afro-American cultural heritage and that they foster the black American's social and political goals. Though numerous writers and critics took issue with specific theories emanating from the Black Arts movement, black American literature was greatly influenced in the sixties by this expression of black power in the arts.

Yet another striking feature of the contemporary scene was the involvement of black women writers in unparalleled numbers. This book is a result of my interest in the emergence of these women writers and, especially, my curiosity about the novelists who preceded them. When and why had black women first begun to write novels? What had these novels been about?

How many black women had written novels prior to the sixties' cultural revolt? Were there unsung geniuses among them? If black women writers responded along with black men to the literary "call to arms" of the Black Arts movement, were the themes and concerns in their stories similar to those of an earlier time? Until fairly recently, and with few exceptions, the body of fiction produced by Afro-American writers had been largely ignored or dismissed by the great majority of literary scholars and critics in whose view the fiction was fundamentally limited by its race consciousness and focus on protest. If race consciousness and protest characterize the work of Afro-American novelists (predominately male) whose work had received the greatest degree of critical attention, did novels written by Afro-American women possess similar flaws? And if so, what could they reveal about the black woman novelist's social and political views? What could one learn precisely by examining these works and the changing nature of their race consciousness, racial protest, and other themes over time?

This book, then, is based on a study of fifty-eight of the sixty-four novels written by black American women between 1891 and 1965. The same questions were asked concerning themes in each novel examined: (1) What areas of concern are expressed, and what is their relevance to specific groups? (2) What viewpoints—social, economic, moral, political—are discussed or disclosed? and (3) What other themes not included above do the novels contain?

Reading and analysis of the novels reveal that a variety of approaches to similar issues characterize the periods 1891–1920, 1921–1945, and 1946–1965. These approaches and these issues are discussed in the first three chapters. Each of these chapters also contains critical analyses of selected novels to illustrate findings concerning the foci of the novelists' major concerns during each period. Whereas the analysis of concerns and issues appearing in the novels involved survey and quantification based on a reading of the novels (see Appendix B), those selected to illustrate these themes were chosen for the depth and artistry with which major concerns are treated.

Chapter I examines *Iola Leroy* by Frances E. W. Harper and *Contending Forces* by Pauline Hopkins and discusses the novelists' use of fiction as a weapon of protest as well as their (as it now appears) curiously innocent attempts at the moral elevation of the nation and of the race.

The second chapter focuses on the race consciousness and self-criticism of the novels written after the First World War. Here, novels by Jessie Fauset—*The Chinaberry Tree* and *Comedy, American Style*—and by Zora Neale Hurston—*Jonah's Gourd-Vine* and *Moses, Man of the Mountain*—illustrate the black woman novelist's concern during this period with intraracial color prejudice, "passing," middle-class values, and most importantly, the ideal of self-help.

Chapter III documents the increasing complexity, sophistication, and maturity of the novels after the Second World War, a period when the novelists, in writing about issues such as discrimination and prejudice, the ghetto and racial integration, created works of universal meaning. These concerns and this development are elaborated in discussions of Ann Petry's *The Narrows*, Paule Marshall's *BrownGirl, Brownstones*, Kristin Hunter's *God Bless the Child*, and Mary E. Vroman's *Esther*.

Chapter IV discusses some of the broad characteristics of Afro-American fiction and compares it to fiction of the American mainstream. The final chapter presents an overall summary of findings.

My hope is that readers will discover, as I did, that novels written by black Americans, especially those by women, constitute much more than a catalog of the race's injuries and grievances. The great majority of these stories had a didactic purpose and an inward focus that has been too little recognized or examined. Extensions of a much older cultural tradition, the stories carry messages of utter seriousness addressed to the novelists' fellow black Americans. Novels by black American women, both in their prescriptive character and in their identity as works of protest, make a special contribution to our understanding of Afro-American social and political thought.

To trace the historical development of these novels as literary works is to watch a wonderful drama unfold. First signalled in the twenties and thirties in Zora Neale Hurston's

short stories and novels, the climax of this development occurs after World War II, when black women novelists in significant numbers successfully addressed the aesthetic problem of creating works of art that are both race-conscious and
universally meaningful. However, an even more compelling
drama is also reflected in these stories. As a body of fiction,
they reveal and document a part of the inner life of an oppressed people. They provide abundant evidence of the complexity and great vitality of the response of black Americans
to the changing circumstances of their lives.

ACKNOWLEDGMENTS

It is a pleasure to thank those who have been especially important to the completion of this project. I am indebted to the faculty of the American Civilization Department at The George Washington University in Washington, D.C. I am especially indebted to Letitia Woods Brown, now deceased, for her generosity, wisdom and example as a teacher and scholar. Likewise, I can never repay Robert H. Walker, a member of the American Civilization faculty at George Washington University and the general editor of the series in which this volume appears. He has been a continuing source of friendship and professional encouragement and provided the crucial guidance for the work upon which this study is based.

I have greatly appreciated the help of staff members at the Library of Congress and of those at the Moorland-Spingarn Research Center at Howard University who befriended me and this project over the years.

I owe thanks to Nathan I. Huggins, Jr., director of the W.E.B. Du Bois Institute for Afro-American Research at Harvard University, who read and offered valuable criticism of the original manuscript. I am pleased to thank my fellow staff members at the National Endowment for the Humanities for their friendly interest in this project. This list would be incomplete without mention of Maben D. Herring, Gretchen G. Fox, and Barbara W. Schecter.

Among others to thank is Joan Davis who typed the manuscript and whose avid interest in its content made her a pleasure to work with. Finally, Joan R. Sealy, Thomas M. Keyes, and my sons will each know why I especially thank them.

PROLOGUE

INTRODUCTION: MORE THAN JUST STORIES

A significant outcome of recent scholarship and public interest in fiction by black American women has been the rediscovery of Zora Neale Hurston's novels. In three of four novels Hurston wrote between 1934 and 1939, *Jonah's Gourd Vine* (1934), *Their Eyes Were Watching God* (1937), and *Moses, Man of the Mountain* (1939), one finds the artistic culmination of a number of important elements traditionally influencing the fiction produced by black American women. The most important of these elements was the novelists' fervent hope that their stories would serve as instruments of racial freedom. The black woman novelist's deeply felt sense of purpose greatly influenced the content of the novels and, more than any other factor, explains their special character. Seizing upon every fictional strategy and rhetorical device at their command, black women novelists, beginning in the 1890s, produced works of social protest and racial appeal based upon Christian and democratic principles. During the final decade of the nineteenth century, their stories challenged the social order then being established in portrayals that refuted the black stereotype, exposed injustice in both the North and South, and, in curious tales about tragic mulattoes, focused attention on the irony and irrationality of the color line.

While literary critics have long recognized, and frequently criticized, the black novel's focus on protest, they have scarcely been aware of its inward focus or of the messages the novels contained that were aimed directly at black folk. Yet, the prescriptiveness, especially of the early novels, is anything but subtle. Black women novelists, with respect to their black audiences, used the stories to advocate race pride and loyalty, morality, and middle-class values, including educational attainment—all for the sake of the racial group. Although the content of race protest in the novels reveals much about how a few members of the aggrieved black minority perceived the oppression of their group, careful study of the novels' prescriptive content, the injunctions to black folk concerning the role that they themselves must play in winning their freedom, can provide insight into the very process of Afro-American cultural development and survival. Indeed, the use of fiction by black women novelists as instruments of protest and of uplift, is itself an example of this process at work. In these novels, many of which were written expressly for the purpose of survival and freedom, we can observe which aspects of the cultural environment black women novelists perceived and chose to promote as efficacious for the welfare of the racial group.

Robert Hemenway, using Zora Neale Hurston's work as an example, addresses the special role of black fiction in Afro-American culture. He points to black fiction's origins in the older Afro-American oral tradition and shows how legends, proverbs, songs, and especially folktales enabled Afro-Americans to endure a history of slavery, oppression, and race prejudice through the development and transmission of a separate African-American culture. "When Black people began to publish novels and short stories in fairly significant numbers during the latter half of the 19th century," according to Hemenway, "the tradition crossed over into written literature, where its positive, heuristic function continued to survive, sometimes by authorial intent, sometimes simply because the tradition was woven into the fabric of the Afro-American experience."[1]

Examination of the Afro-American experience indicates that

the folktale is part of the ancient heritage of Afro-American culture and that its primary function has been one of education. Lawrence Levine, author of *Black Culture and Black Consciousness*, writes that Afro-Americans equated folktales with education during and after the period of slavery. In the primacy of its didactic role and in its refusal to countenance a romantic view of the world, the contemporary Afro-American folktale differs from other aspects of black culture's oral expressive tradition. Its deadly serious purpose was the sharing of knowledge about forces shaping the world of Afro-Americans and providing instruction in withstanding and/or overcoming those forces.[2]

Among the most potent forces shaping the world of black Americans during the 1890s when numbers of black women began to write novels were the crystallization and spread of racist thought and the institutionalization of a new racial caste system. By the turn of the century, Americans widely believed black Americans to be an alien and degenerate population in the country's midst, an inherently benighted race that could never be assimilated into the nation's social or political life. They believed that black people could never be fully civilized irrespective of even heroic effort at their uplift through educational and/or religious training.

Because black women novelists themselves viewed moral uplift during this period as part of the strategy of survival, their novels, similar to most contemporary black folktales, were concerned with inculcating "a vision of the good and moral life." While they were ostensibly concerned with the race's spiritual welfare, the stories definitely had a "practical cast" and must be understood within the context of the life situation of the slave and freedman.[3] This utilitarianism characterizes, as well, the novels written by black women in the post–World War I period when the exemplums in the stories conveyed middle-class, rather than Christian, values.

Black women's novels prior to the Second World War are, above all, mindful of the racial group. The voice of protest in the novels is not typically that of the author speaking as an individual but that of a black writer speaking out on behalf of the racial group. Similarly, the moral of the story intended for black audiences is carried most often through the experiences and fortunes of black characters whose situation is meant to be taken as representative, not by way of tales focusing on the idiosyncratic fate of highly individuated heroes and heroines. In this broad sense, the stories black women wrote reflect their perception of social reality and are not simply the products of the writer's literary imagination.

A number of the novelists, however, meant their stories to stand only as testimonies of personal survival. In these fictionalized accounts of the authors' own experiences, the writer's first concern was to leave a record of that which she herself had endured. These stories vary according to whether the writer perceived her audience as black and/or white. In a number of these stories, the self as Alexander Butterfield describes it in his *Black Autobiography* is very much in evidence: a self "conceived as a member of an oppressed social group, with ties and responsibilities to other members, a conscious political identity, drawing sustenance from the past experience of the group, giving back the iron of endurance fashioned into armor and weapons for the use of the next generation of fighters."[4]

Although most of the novelists who wrote stories based closely on the drama of their personal experiences were cognizant of their ties to the racial group and of the influence of race upon their lives, for many inspiration of their fellows was an important, though secondary, motive. For these novelists, a number of whom resorted to vanity presses in order to have their stories published, an indomitable determination to tell their own story for their own sake led them to write.

Harriet Wilson's *Our Nig*, the first novel known to have been written by a black American in the United States, is autobiographical. Wilson's story tells of her virtual enslavement and cruel treatment in the home of a Northern white family. Wilson wrote the novel and had it published herself in the hope of selling enough copies to pay the medical costs for treatment of her seriously ill son. An appendix to the novel contains letters from several of Wilson's acquaintances, which provide additional information about Wilson's life and attest to the truth of her tale. "Truth is stranger than fiction," wrote one friend who signed herself simply "Allida." "She was indeed a slave, in every sense of the word; and a lonely one, too," wrote another, more than likely a white woman, named Margaret Thorn.[5]

This novel, which apparently heralded the tradition of novel writing by Afro-Americans in the United States, combines elements of the slave narrative and conventions of the sentimental novel.[6] It shares with the great majority of later novels by black American women a strong impulse to testify against the country's ill treatment of black Americans. Like most stories written by black women around the turn of the century, *Our Nig*, which recounts the experiences of the orphaned girl Frado, stresses Northern prejudice and racism. *Our Nig* is also similar to novels black women wrote thirty-two years later in that the questions Wilson poses in the character of Frado about her mistreatment are framed in terms of elementary Christian principles. Yet, in spite of the novel's concern with race prejudice, *Our Nig* is primarily the tale of a single individual. The novel does not draw upon those nourishing aspects of a common Afro-American culture which fostered in later black women novelists a growing sense of group identity and a powerful desire to communicate through fiction with the black community.

The great majority of black women's novels are infused with this sense of racial corporateness. The central concern of their stories is the welfare of the race as a group; their novels are vitally engaged, therefore, with threats to Afro-American culture as well as with that which concerns American blacks as individuals. Zora Neale Hurston's triumph was to be the first black woman novelist to succeed in incorporating into her stories the "imaginative strategies," content, and didactic goals of the Afro-American oral tradition.[7] Partly as a result of her childhood in the all-black town of Eatonville, Florida, her training as an anthropologist, and her own artistry, Hurston was able to produce works of art which reflected her belief that, irrespective of the actions of the larger society, Afro-American liberation and freedom were dependent upon the black community's recognition of the folk heritage that sustains and binds it together. This heritage Hurston viewed as an essential form of communication, a still viable means for adjudicating group values and for achieving wise group decision making. One of the most prolific of black women novelists of her day, Hurston was herself a committed participant in this process.

While Zora Neale Hurston is a landmark figure among black women novelists, black women writers in ever increasing numbers, especially after the Second World War, produced work that is race conscious, yet notable for its aesthetic achievement. Taken together, these novels by black American women provide insight into a great deal more than how a select number of black women have apprehended their world. Their stories are remarkable traceries of part of the process by which Afro-American culture has been transmitted and is being continually transformed in the interest of Afro-American survival and freedom.

Notes

1. Hemenway, "Hurston's Buzzards and Elijah's Ravens," 38. (All noted titles are cited in full in the Bibliography. Titles are included in notes only to distinguish between several works by a single author.)
2. Levine, 115, 34.
3. Ibid., 97.
4. Butterfield, Introd., 3.
5. Wilson, 138–40.
6. Ibid., lii.
7. Hemenway, 32.

I

"I HAVE WOVEN A STORY . . .": UPLIFT AND PROTEST, 1891–1920

The development of Afro-American fiction proceeded very gradually from its inception in the mid-nineteenth century. Harriet Wilson's *Our Nig*, the first novel to be published in the United States by a black American, appeared in 1859 when the great majority of Afro-Americans were still enslaved. While other and perhaps earlier novels by black Americans are certain to be discovered eventually, it now appears that a thirty-two-year hiatus occurred before another black woman—Emma Dunham Kelly—published a novel in the United States.

In the 1890s, however, a number of novels written by black women began to appear. These early works fall solidly within the category of purpose fiction. Written to serve a social and/or religious purpose, the novels emerged during a time when the black American community, under the pressure of post-Reconstruction oppression and a solidifying caste system, was struggling on many fronts to gain control of its social and political life. The overt violence against persons of African descent, the legally sanctioned denial of their citizenship rights, the growth of both formal and informal structures of segregation and barriers to the Afro-American's free and fair participation in society and the nation's economy, and finally, the untrammeled spread of anti-Negro propaganda throughout every level of society led historian Rayford Logan to term the period of the 1890s "the nadir" of Afro-American history.

Yet, it was during this decade when the black American was apparently friendless—abandoned by government, the courts, former abolitionists, and Northern liberals—that the beginnings of an organized self-help movement within the race emerged.[1] Most of the novels written by black women during this period were part of the group response of black Americans to the social and political imperatives that brought the self-help movement into being. From this point in their history, the great majority of black women's novels reveal the novelists' fidelity to the race-conscious ideals enunciated during this period. In these early novels, ideas of self-help find expression in themes of race loyalty, race uplift, and protest. While the self-help ideal greatly influenced the content of the novels until the close of the Second World War, the stories written by black women prior to World War I, in their explicit assertion of an ethical framework based on Christian religion and principles, can be clearly distinguished from those published during the post–World War I period.[2]

Race Loyalty and Spiritual Uplift

Novels written by black women between 1891 and 1920 focus to a greater or lesser degree on religious behavior and values.[3] Most of the stories either posit or assume a direct relationship between the widespread practice of Christianity and the social and political uplift of American blacks. In only two novels of the period, Emma Kelly's *Megda* and Amelia Johnson's *The Hazeley Family*, do the novelists advocate Christian morality for the spiritual well-being of the individual. In these stories, neither Johnson nor Kelly expresses concern with broad social issues or with the role of the individual in society. Other black women novelists who published between 1891 and 1920 saw in Protestant Christianity not only a system of personal ethics but also the blueprint for a just society. In their insistent appeals to the nation's Christian conscience and in their attempts to arouse a sense of moral outrage regarding new forms of oppression, black women novelists acted upon an immediatist philosophy resembling that of the later abolitionists. Their stories attest to the continued vitality of antebellum, moral suasionism which the novelists now used as a conscious strategy of racial self-defense.[4] Even protest novels of the period in which the tone of protest is muted, as in Sarah Fleming's *Hope's Highway* and Zara Wright's *Black and White Tangled Threads* and *Kenneth*, make their arguments based on America's failure to adhere to its Christian, not its democratic, principles.

In addition, the stories written by black women novelists, especially in the 1890s, express the conviction that the nation along with its black citizens has been morally damaged by slavery. Evidence of America's damaged public conscience, according to the novelists, was manifested in the triumph of materialistic values after the Civil War and in the country's inhumane and violent treatment of black Americans after Reconstruction. Frances E. W. Harper wrote in *Iola Leroy*:

Both races have reacted on each other—man fettered the slave and cramped their own souls; denied him knowledge, and darkened their spiritual insight.
A people cannot habitually trample on law and justice without retrograding toward barbarism.
Because there are rights more sacred than rights of property and superior intelligence . . . you cannot willingly deprive the negro of a single right as a citizen without sending demoralization through your own ranks.[5]

While men and women of both races need spiritual elevation, the novelists contended, the Afro-American was forced to bear the burden of the white man's sin—a burden of poverty, ignorance, and low estate. The mulatto was an especially visible and galling reminder of the impact upon the Afro-American family of the white man's moral dissolution. "Emancipation has done much, but time and moral training among the white men of the South are the only cures for concubinage," Pauline Hopkins declared.[6]

Like other Afro-American thinkers of the period, Hopkins viewed the race question as a simple matter of ethical principle. "Politics nor statesmanship can help the Negro," she claimed, "because the problem is one of ethics."[7] Similarly, W.E.B. Du Bois, in a lecture delivered in 1907 and entitled "Religion in the South" blamed the segregated white church for the low state of Negro morality. Prejudiced, white Christians, having refused to minister to the Negro's spiritual needs, could not justly reproach the black man for his moral deficits, Du Bois claimed. "It is a problem not simply of political expediency, of economic success, but a problem above all of religious and social life; and it carries with it not simply a demand for its own solution, but beneath it lies the whole question of the real intent of our civilization: Is the civilization of the United States Christian?"[8]

While education of the American social conscience is a dominant theme in the strongest novels of the period, the novels treat the moral education of black Americans with nearly equal fervor.[9]

The novelists' concern with the moral status of the black population resulted, in part, from the growing practice of lynching and from the proliferation of anti-Negro propaganda in hundreds of newspapers, magazines, novels, sermons, and questionable scientific works by scholars.[10] In this hostile atmosphere, which involved serious debate about whether or not the black race was fully human and which at its most extreme justified legal and extralegal measures to keep black people rigidly controlled on the premise that especially black men were prone to behave as sexual savages and beasts, black women novelists argued for flawless morality on the part of all black Americans. Because they believed it to be crucial for racial survival, they charged Afro-Americans with their moral obligation to be positive factors in the struggle for survival and freedom.[11]

Black women novelists sought to address the question of Negro humanity, and hence the very capacity of the black individual for morality, by writing romantic tales focused on black heroes and heroines of saintlike virtue. Significantly, all of the heroes and heroines that appear in the race novels written before the First World War are fair-skinned mulattoes.[12] These near-white characters, which the novelists invariably depicted as exemplary figures, were deliberately drawn to serve as models which embodied the novelists' ideals of morality, success, and race loyalty. These figures, in addition, served as counter-stereotypes with whom white readers could identify.

There was yet another reason why black women novelists chose not to portray Afro-Americans of realistic human dimensions. They refused to allow any hint of spiritual imperfection in a black character and thereby concede the possibility of an inherent flaw in the racial character because, during this period, the idea of black spiritual inferiority was especially abhorrent to the novelists themselves. Like other Afro-Americans of their day, the novelists appear to have believed that discrimination against a morally inferior people was just. "Ordained intellectual and moral inferiority is the only valid justification of political and social subordination," Kelly Miller, an early black sociologist, declared.[13] As propagandists, black women and other writers of the period attempted to demonstrate the black man's moral equality with whites, and they tried to expose and discredit the rationalizations that had supported slavery and which then lent support to prejudice and discrimination. At the same time, black writers tried, as well, to repair the intellectual and moral harm to the race which resulted from slavery and post–Reconstruction oppression. "The Negro has come handicapped into life and is now on trial before the world," a youth in Frances Harper's *Iola Leroy* declares.[14] The heroine in Zara Wright's *Black and White Tangled Threads* castigates white churchmen for leading their congregations in prayer for the "degraded race of Negroes." Everywhere men in authority denigrate Negroes—in the press and on the platform, she says, leading the black man to know that "every man's hand is against him." The effort of black Americans to combat the wholesale assault on Negro character is exemplified in the "Oath of Afro-American Youth," a pledge that appears in the preface to Kelly Miller's *Out of the House of Bondage*:

I will never bring disgrace upon my race . . . I will live a clean, decent, manly life; I will in all these ways aim to uplift my race so that to everyone bound to it by ties of blood, it shall become a bond of ennoblement and not a byword of reproach.[15]

Afro-American character as depicted in the early novels is impeccably moral, courageous, and intelligent. For example, Iola Leroy, heroine of Harper's novel of the same name; the wife in Zara Wright's *Black and White Tangled Threads*; the young physician in Wright's sequel, *Kenneth*; the educators in Fleming's *Hope's Highway* are all surpassingly upright and noble. Black women described in the stories are as morally flawless as the heroine in Emma Kelly's *Megda*, one of the raceless novels of the period. Megda's physical beauty and ladylike conduct perfectly mirror her purity of soul. "To look and act the 'perfect lady' was Megda's idea of perfection itself." He "was most favorably impressed with the laughing, light-hearted girl, who, however much she laughed and chattered, never once went beyond the bonds of propriety."[16] One-sided, unrealistic characterizations such as these reflect not just the Puritan/Victorian ideals of their creators but also are reverse reflections of the offensive racial stereotype the novels were designed to refute.

Frances Harper, like other thoughtful Afro-Americans of her day, sincerely believed that decent Americans would not knowingly allow the oppression of other decent people. Her novel, therefore, is replete with positive images of black Americans and it also presents models of behavior to be emulated by them. Harper wrote in the closing note of the novel:

I have woven a story whose mission will not be in vain if it awakens in the hearts of our countrymen a stronger sense of justice and a more Christlike humanity. . . . Nor will it be in vain if it inspires the children of that new era to determine that they will embrace every opportunity, develop every faculty, use every power God has given them to rise in the scale of character and condition, to add their quota of good citizenship to the best welfare of the nation.[17]

Harper's writing of an inspirational protest novel, while thought to be unprecedented at the time of its creation and for years afterward, is of a piece with her other proselytizing activities. Throughout a long career, she spoke frequently before black and white audiences throughout the country as an active member of the AME Church, member of the Anti-Slavery

Society of Maine, and representative for the Women's Christian Temperance Union. The most popular black poet of her day, she often included readings of her poetry in her lectures.

In his introduction to *Iola Leroy*, William Grant Still, compiler of the Underground Railroad Records (1872), praised Harper for her work in Negro uplift, citing her concern with temperance, morality, industry, and education. He praised her for having written what he believed to be the first novel published in the United States by an Afro-American woman. Describing *Iola Leroy* as instructive as well as entertaining, he recommended it to churches in the South for use as a Sunday school text. "The grand and ennobling sentiments," he opined, "which have characterized all her [Harper's] utterances in laboring for the elevation of the oppressed will not be found missing in this book."[18]

Harper believed spiritual uplift to be a matter concerning not only black Americans; she saw the Afro-American presence as a special gift and challenge to America.[19] Because the nation had been morally stained by slavery, its spiritual redemption lay in dealing justly with its Negro citizens. In this manner only could America be restored to a state of grace. And, thought Harper, if black men and women could themselves truly understand the irony of the Beatitudes, they too would be freed of slavery's shame.

Has the negro been poor and homeless? The birds of the air had nests and the foxes had holes, but the Son of man had not where to lay His head. Has our name been a synonym of contempt? "He shall be called a Nazarene." *To-day that cross of shame is a throne of power.* Those robes of scorn have changed to habiliments of light, and that crown of mockery to a diadem of glory.[20]

Spiritual uplift was central to race uplift in Harper's view. She believed that spiritual values were at the heart of true education and that, without them social, educational, or political achievements were empty. "Our greatest need, is not more wealth and learning," she wrote, "but a religion replete with life and glowing with love. Let this be the impelling force in the race and it cannot fail to rise in the scale of character and condition."[21]

Harper did not hesitate to demand of Afro-Americans that each participate in the work of uplift, an effort that required moral rectitude and unselfish commitment in the Christlike manner of missionaries and martyrs. Again and again in *Iola Leroy* she stresses the ethical nature of the black man and woman's responsibility to the race. Major conflicts in the novel concern issues of loyalty—to race, family, and friends. One of the novel's central themes is that loyalty to these groups is invariably ennobling and morally correct. Mulattoes and near-white Negroes especially, she writes, must remain steadfast in their commitment to the Negro group. When Iola's brother Harry learns of their Negro parentage, he is stunned but finds the courage after a time to enlist in an all-Negro Civil War regiment. The sentiments he expresses after undergoing the terrible struggles brought on by his new knowledge are echoed later in the tale by another young mulatto who says, "I think it would be treason, not only to the race, but to humanity, to have you ignoring your kindred and masquerading as a white man."[22] In fact, Iola Leroy's two rejections of the enchanting but white Dr. Gresham are yet more emphatic statements of the race-loyalty theme. When declining Gresham's marriage proposal, she says, "I don't think I could best serve my race by forsaking them and marrying you. . . . I must serve the race which needs me most."[23] Iola, relinquishing her chance to escape from the race through marriage to a kind and courageous man, remains in the South. After the war, she selflessly teaches in a freedmen's school, while simultaneously undertaking a tireless search for her Negro relatives. Years later, Frank Lattimer, her fiancé, marvels at Iola's dedication and loyalty to the race:

I know a young lady who could have cast her lot with the favored race, yet chose to take her place with freed people, as their teacher, friend, and adviser. This young lady was alone in the world. She had been fearfully wronged, and to her stricken heart came a brilliant offer of love, home, and social position. But she bound her heart to the mast of duty, closed her ears to the siren song, and could not be lured from her purpose.[24]

In a curious way, the love story of Iola and Frank Lattimer, which takes place after the Leroy family is reunited and has moved to the North, expresses Harper's predominant concerns with morality, race loyalty, and uplift. Each lover is attracted to the other's unflagging dedication to race betterment. Each appreciates the moral crisis the other had to confront in the past—a crisis that involved a choice of escaping from or retaining his or her racial identity. As Iola's affection for Lattimer deepens, she begins to see him as magnificent as her Old Testament heroes, biblical figures like Moses and Nehemiah who "put aside their own advantages for their race and country." Having refused the worldly advantages of racial disaffiliation, Lattimer becomes the embodiment of Iola's ideal of a "high, heroic, manhood." Lattimer's rejection of his white grandmother's offer to make him heir to her estate provided he renounce his Afro-American heritage is analagous to Iola's refusal to marry Gresham. To remain within the race, Iola says, is a privilege higher than any conferred by wealth or social position; it is a priceless honor to labor for the race's uplifting.[25]

Harper's exhortative tone as expressed in these passages is pervasive in the novel and reaches its height in the story's tender love scenes. For example, in answer to Lattimer's solicitous inquiry about her pensive mood at one point in the story, Iola reveals that she is thinking about a recent lynching and that never far from her thoughts is her great concern about the condition of her people. Because their affection springs from a mutual desire to serve their race, Lattimer understands completely. Their "hearts beat in loving unison. One grand noble purpose was giving tone and color to their lives and strengthening the bonds of affection between them."[26] Harper stresses the race loyalty/self-help theme even in the engagement scene in which the lovers' promise of lifelong commitment to each other also signals their joint commitment to the race: "His words were more than a tender strain wooing her to love and happiness, they were a clarion call to a life of high and holy worth, a call which found a response in her heart."[27]

Harper abruptly abandons dramatic elaboration of the novel's main themes once Iola and Lattimer are married. The final scenes in the story take place at a formal gathering, a *conversazione*, at the home of Dr. Stillman, a character based on William Grant Still. While at the gathering, the educated and privileged members of the black middle class discuss practical approaches to race uplift. Harper uses this technique, although with little finesse, to express her strong conviction that rigorous, personal morality on the part of black Americans is crucial to racial advancement. Stillman's guests of the evening agree that strict moral self-discipline is the best armor against oppression and that pleasure-seeking for its own sake is a threat to the Negro's soul, manhood, and destiny. This extended discussion in the novel reveals Harper's utter distaste for the youthful joy and abandon that are such obviously missing elements in the novel's love stories. One guest declares: "We must instill [the idea] into our young people that the true strength of a race means purity in women and uprightness in men; who can say, with Sir Galahad:—'My strength is the strength of ten, Because my heart is pure.' "[28] Another reads a poem titled "A Rallying Cry," which captures these same attitudes:

> Oh, children of the tropics,
>   Amid our pain and wrong
> Have you no other mission
>   Than music, dance, and song?
> When through the weary ages
>   Our dripping tears still fall,
> Is this a time to dally
>   With pleasure's silken thrall?. . .
>
> Dream not of ease or pleasure,
>   Nor honor wealth nor fame
> Till from the dust you've lifted
>   Our long-dishonored name.[29]

In the same vein in one of the novel's minor themes, Harper condemns the use of alcohol. Because she viewed alcohol as another threat to the black man and woman's freedom, she compares Southern saloon keepers who cater to the black trade to antebellum slave catchers.[30] The refusal of American politicians to address the temperance issue satisfactorily, she claimed, was analogous to their long refusal to acknowledge the evil of slavery: "We have had two evils by which our obedience to law has been tested," she wrote. " 'I beliebs we might be a people if it warn't for dat mizzable drink,' " a freedman in the novel exclaims.[31] In another scene, a freedman upon finding his long-lost mother after years of searching after the end of the Civil War, refuses an innocent offer of homemade wine to celebrate the occasion: "Let the wine go sour, and everyone sign the pledge," he cries.[32]

At the close of *Iola Leroy*, Stillman's guests conclude that not only the race but America itself presents a fine field for missionary endeavor. This is the novel's final message. As unworthy as the black man's pursuit of pleasure in a time of crisis is America's blind pursuit of empire and wealth. It is not God's will that His favored nation pass through the moral crisis of slavery only to abandon its spiritual values. Yet, the conjoined future of America and of its Negro citizenry could be viewed optimistically, for noble men and women of color, while serving their race, would indirectly help repair the nation's conscience. With the help of God, they would help make possible "a far higher and better Christian civilization than our country has ever known!"[33]

Racial Protest

Racial protest is a major element in the fiction of the period; indeed, it was the deplorable state of post–Reconstruction race relations that brought the self-help movement and this body of fiction into being. While the narratives focus primarily on the lives of privileged mulatto characters, the stories are suffused, nonetheless, with the hard facts of Negro existence. Frances Harper's *Iola Leroy*, Pauline Hopkins' *Contending Forces*, Sara Lee Fleming's *Hope's Highway*, and Zara Wright's *Black and White Tangled Threads* and *Kenneth* each stress the precariousness of Afro-American life resulting from racial violence. In *Kenneth*, the life and career of a young black physician are threatened by the romantic overtures of a spoiled and willful white patient. In their novels, both Hopkins and Harper indicate that lynching is a postslavery, post–Civil War phenomenon. Both adamantly reject the claim that lynching stemmed from the outrage of decent men at the rape of white women by black men. Rather, these writers charged that the practice of lynching was a new expression of the Old Southern spirit of racial oppression. Hopkins wrote:

Lynching does not stop crime; it is but a subterfuge for killing men. . . .

No; it is not rape. If the Negro votes, he is shot; if he marries a white woman, he is shot; if he accumulates property, he is shot or lynched—he is a pariah whom the national government cannot defend.[34]

Black women novelists contended that the social, economic, and political progress of black Americans threatened white supremacy and that this was the true cause of lynching. Despite protestations regarding the need to control the black man because of his essentially animalistic nature, lynching "was instituted to crush the manhood of the enfranchised black."[35]

In addressing the issue of lynching, black women novelists seized the moral offensive. To charges of Negro criminality and rape, they flung the countercharge of rape, citing the white man's exploitation and abuse of Negro women.

The Afro-American heroine retains her virtue against great odds in these early stories. For example, Sappho Clark, the heroine in *Contending Forces*, is kidnapped, raped, and impregnated before she is fifteen. Hopkins writes in the novel:

Merciful God! Irony of ironies! *The men who created the mulatto race, who recruit its ranks year after year by the very means which they invoked lynch law to suppress, bewailing the sorrows of violated womanhood!*[36]

Black women novelists viewed the sexual abuse of black women by white men as an attack on the integrity of the Afro-American family and deleterious, therefore, to the race's future.[37] The horror of Hopkins' convoluted and rambling twelve-part tale, *Of One Blood*, is the brother-sister incest that takes place because the young people involved are unaware they have a parent in common, a white man.

Such havoc is wrought by evil deeds. The first doomed step of an individual or a nation, who can tell where it will end, through what dark and doleful shades of hell the soul must pass in travail?[38]

On the other hand, black women novelists protested against antimiscegenation laws in the novels. They charged that laws against interracial marriage had the effect of denying legal protection to thousands of black women and their children.[39] Because antimiscegenation statutes ruled such marriages illegal, the children born of such unions were illegitimate, thus increasing by the thousands those within the Afro-American group who were designated social outcasts and misfits.

In several early stories, black women novelists defended the character and honor of mulattoes, especially of women. Their defense of the mulatto was aimed as much toward prejudiced black Americans as toward whites.[40]

Although most of the stories written from 1891 to 1920 can be characterized as protest novels, some were more conciliatory in tone than others. An attitude of conciliation rather than of angry remonstrance is particularly evident in Fleming's *Hope's Highway* and Wright's *Black and White Tangled Threads*. Fleming and Wright, similar to Harper and Hopkins, argued, albeit cautiously, for equitable educational opportunities for black Americans. Both believed education to be a primary means to race uplift and condemned those forces which sought to keep the Negro ignorant.

In general, the novels of the period do not focus on the relationship between educational repression and the Afro-American's socioeconomic status. Instead, the novelists take positions along a spectrum vividly set forth in the Booker T. Washington–W.E.B. Du Bois debate about the virtues of vocational training versus liberal education. Their stories ask whether or not acceptance of Washington's accommodationist position also implies acceptance of the idea of the black man or woman's lesser humanity and whether or not Washington's social policy, even if successful, requires partial sacrifice of black

men and women's full citizenship rights. Frances Harper and
Pauline Hopkins—the most assertive of the novelists—agreed
with Du Bois. Both insisted that black Americans were obli-
gated as citizens and as men and women to protest vigorously
against racial injustice. In *Contending Forces*, therefore, Hopkins raises a cry not only against racial oppression but also
against what she saw as the self-inflicted compromises of black
accommodationists.

Contending Forces, a stark melodrama which compares the
brutalities of post–Reconstruction America to that of the South
during the slavery era, is the most forceful protest novel written by a black American woman prior to Ann Petry's *The
Street*.[41] In addition to protesting racial injustice, *Contending
Forces* mounts a strong argument in favor of a policy of militant protest on the part of Afro-Americans. In the novel, Hopkins attacks the nostalgic and romantic aura surrounding the
slavery era and, at the same time, exposes the moral bank-
ruptcy of the post–Reconstruction South. She claims in the
story that identical impulses produced the institution of slavery and the pattern of racial adjustment that developed after
the war. One of her immediate aims was to destroy that sympathy for the white South which had led Northern liberals to
abandon the cause of the black man and woman to Southern
will.

The question of disfranchisement has speedily resolved itself into one
of serfdom; that means a gradual resumption of all the relations of
slavery, with, perhaps the exception of the auction block, which in
the end will also return for short periods, for the punishment of minor offenses.[42]

Pauline Hopkins seized upon the weapon of protest fiction, because she was convinced that the race could best defend itself
by "using the very methods of the South . . . [by creating]
sentiment for the race and against its detractors."[43] In *Contending Forces*, she wrote a polemical melodrama portraying
good and evil in starkest contrast. She shamelessly exploited
other conventions of melodrama to lend force to the novel's
protest themes. Her schematization of characters into dual

alignments of good and evil also characterizes her treatment of the plot. In its overall design, the story portrays and compares the actual conditions of Negro life prior to and just after the Civil War with those portrayed in postbellum, proslavery fiction. Hopkins, in addition, contrasts the flaccid Northern response to post–Reconstruction racial oppression to the indefatigable crusade for Negro freedom waged by abolitionists before the war.

The tale begins obliquely. Charles Montfort, an immensely wealthy planter, emigrates from Bermuda to America to avoid Britain's newly passed antislavery law. A kind and enlightened master, Montfort plans to free his slaves but in such a manner as to preserve his wealth. His liberal views, however, quickly undermine the stunning social success of his family's initial weeks in Newbern, North Carolina, his family's new American home. Before the endangered family can relocate in Bermuda, Montfort is killed in cold blood on the front porch of his home by Newbern's "committee on public safety." His young and gracious wife, whom the townsfolk suspect of possessing a trace of Negro blood, is stripped, tied to a post, and lashed until she is unconscious. Grace Montfort and her children are subsequently sold into slavery. The fate of the children and that of their descendants is unraveled later in the narrative.

In the title of the novel's second chapter, "The Days 'Before the War,' " Hopkins alludes both to these violent initial events in the story and to the myth-laden South of postbellum, proslavery fiction. The irony of the title is underscored as the novel unfolds. Hopkins shows the prevalence of indiscriminant cruelty at every level of antebellum Southern society, a pervasive cruelty that encompassed whites of the lowest caste as well as those of the aristocracy. Grace Montfort, who initially had been considered a flower of upper-class womanhood, becomes the property of Jackson Pollock, the man responsible for her husband's death. Pollock, when he is thwarted in his attempt to make Grace his mistress when she commits suicide, then lays claim to her unwilling maid. He presses one of Montfort's children into servitude as his personal valet. In the crudest vernacular, two lower-class white men at one point in the chapter discuss recent events—a successful lynching, a raffle in which the first prize is a mulatto breeder, the accidental shooting of a dog trained to track runaways. One man confides to his friend: "Ef it'd been the nigger I'd happened ter kill, hit would'a been all right." Hopkins insists that upperclass Southerners collude and even take a leading role in antiblack violence. Hank Davis and Bill Sampson are but pawns of the socially prominent Anson Pollock, the secret head of Newbern's Klan-like Committee on Policy Safety.

In such a milieu, white men and women can escape neither the guilt of slavery nor recognition of their own vulnerability. The murder of Charles Montfort is not legally redressed. Montfort's land is legally confiscated, his wife and children legally swallowed by slavery. Another white man, whose tale is told in a brief vignette in the same chapter, is caught while attempting to escape to Canada with his mulatto girlfriend, whom he had hoped to marry there. He is sentenced to receive fifty lashes upon being brought to trial. Other vignettes, however, pale when compared with the scene depicting the whipping of Montfort's wife, Grace. Surely it is this scene in the novel which impelled an early critic of Afro-American fiction to object to what he considered the novel's sensationalism. The "exaggeration of *Appointed*," wrote Vernon Loggins, "is nothing compared to the wild portrayal in *Contending Forces*."[44] Yet, Hopkins insisted that the novel's opening chapters were based on fact. She claimed in an advertisment in the *Colored American Magazine* that evidence proving the events in the initial chapters actually occurred could be examined at the Newbern, North Carolina, courthouse and "at the seat of government at Washington, D.C."[45]

In the opening chapters of *Contending Forces*, Hopkins challenges the benevolent view of slavery depicted in proslavery fiction and sets forth her own point of view: slavery was inevitably cruel; to some degree, whites also were inescapably vulnerable within the system; moral degradation usually accompanied the slaveholder's absolute power. In the second half of the novel, which takes place in the post–Reconstruction North, Hopkins focuses on the issue of black protest. Montfort's descendants, now the Smith family, establish themselves comfortably in Boston. As the second section opens, news of yet another lynching in the South galvanizes Boston's Negro community. In response to pleas from Southern Negroes that "Massachusetts let its voice be heard," the Colored American League calls a meeting to determine what action it should take. The narrative at this point poses the questions: What is the true cause of lynching? and, What is the proper response of Northerners, black and white, to lynching and to the general mistreatment of black men and women in the South?

A conversation between a Massachusetts state representative, the Honorable Herbert Clapp, and John Langley, a well-to-do black lawyer, dramatizes the tendency of Northern politicians to sacrifice the cause of the Southern Negro in the interest of political expediency. Both Clapp and Langley agree that each will benefit if members of the Colored American League agree to a policy of moderation in their response to lynching. The encounter between the two men, however, is not amicable. Langley compares the post–Reconstruction response of Northern politicians to Judas' betrayal of Christ. Clapp acknowledges the truth of his charge but retorts without apology: "But the South, man!" exclaimed the Colonel, pounding on the table: "The South has rights as well as you. They are *white men*, man; you can't expect us to leave them out."[46] Yet, Langley, like Clapp, betrays black people, too. In return for the meager crumbs of a city appointment and control over a few patronage jobs, he agrees to use all of his influence to blunt any activist stirrings that might develop at the meeting of the league. Sealing their unholy bargain, Langley says: "You may be the best we can do, and the best is d—n poor. Colonel, you just make up your mind to one thing. It's going to cost you something; yes, sir, right smart."[47]

In her sympathetic portrayal of Arthur Lewis, an honest servant of his race who bears a striking resemblance to Booker T. Washington, Hopkins casts further doubt on the moderate approach to social protest. Lewis is a dedicated principal of a manual training school for black youth in the South. He not only believes Negroes should not vote until well prepared for citizenship through education and training but that Negro criminality causes lynching and that Northern publicity about the practice is dangerously inflamatory. A full-fledged accommodationist, Lewis believes that the protest tactic should be abandoned because it harms the Southern Negro cause. According to Lewis, black people must eschew efforts to win political equality; they must commit themselves instead to a program of self-help focused on vocational training. Lewis' message to those assembled at the meeting of the Colored American League to discuss Massachusetts' response to the lynching is that many men like himself are working in the South. These men "have planned that with the aid of our universities we shall root out evil and ignorance and in the future give our race a clean pure citizenship . . . politics is the bane of the Negro's existence."[48]

Other speakers in turn argue for a moderate approach to protesting the lynching when a stranger suddenly takes his place upon the platform. The stranger opens his remarks with Patrick Henry's ringing cry, "Gentlemen may cry 'peace,' but there is not peace." The stranger then eloquently compares the post–Reconstruction crusade for racial justice to the antislavery crusade and to the struggle for American independence. His lofty rhetoric as well as the tragic tale he tells are forceful and convincing. His powerful argument for militant protest sweeps aside the uneasy consensus that had obtained prior to his appearance. Having been half persuaded by arguments counseling passivity in the face of outrageous injustice, the league is restored by his speech to its former sense of high purpose in pursuit of a race-centered mission.

Hopkins was herself convinced that only a sustained, moral outcry in a campaign similar to that waged by the abolitionists could defeat lynching and racial injustice. Neither counterforce nor a gradualist policy, she believed, could bring about change in the treatment of black Americans. A character in *Contending Forces* states: "My friends, it is going to take time to straighten out this problem; it will only be done by the formation of public opinion. Brute force will not accomplish anything. We must *agitate*. As the anti-slavery apostles went everywhere preaching the word fifty years before emancipation, *so must we do to-day*."[49]

In the novel, William Smith is the fictional counterpart of

W.E.B. Du Bois. Smith is as idealistic and headstrong as Arthur Lewis, a thinly disguised Booker T. Washington, is earnest and cautious. Smith dreams of starting a free school for black youth that will embrace "every known department of science," while Lewis heads a manual training school in the South. The two young friends are each engaged to a young woman who agrees with his point of view. Will's fiancée, Sappho, of course, is far lovelier than Lewis' fiancée, Dora. Like Will, Sappho sees no alternative to militant protest. She believes that black people will eventually demand their complete freedom with or without the benefits of a complete education: "The time will come, when our men will grow away from the trammels of narrow prejudice and desire the same treatment that is accorded to other men. Why one can but see that any degree of education and development will not fail of such a result."[50]

Hopkins accomplishes her serious goals in writing the novel—racial protest and advocacy of militant protest by black Americans—in the first two sections of the story. Thereafter, she abandons these themes and the story becomes an exercise in pure entertainment. Melodramatic conventions in the final section, an arch-villain and a heroine in distress, no longer support the social viewpoints or racial policies she initially presents.

John Langley, the black lawyer whose perfidy is exposed in the encounter with Herbert Clapp, is revealed to be a descendant of Anson Pollock, the man who years before had murdered Charles Montfort, who precipitated Grace Montfort's suicide, and who enslaved the Montfort children. Because Langley wants Sappho Clark for himself, he threatens to ruin her impending marriage to Will Smith by revealing her true identity. Langley has discovered that Sappho is actually Mabelle Beaubean of New Orleans. He knows that before the war, when she was a young girl, she was kidnapped, raped, and impregnated by a relative who planned to force her into a life of prostitution. At this point in the story, the novel gratuitously reiterates Hopkins' views concerning slavery's evils, including the burden of the past borne by former slaves and their children, and the respectability and unsullied sexual virtue of the great majority of female mulattoes. The novel closes with a series of implausible coincidences in which Sappho, Will, and all of Charles Montfort's descendants are happily reunited.

Notes

1. While Afro-Americans were engaged in self-help activities before the 1890s, these years saw remarkable growth in Negro institutional life. There was great activity and growth in fraternal and benefit-aid societies. The Afro-American church began to function increasingly as a social welfare agency. The National Association of Colored Women was established in 1892 and took for its motto "Lifting as we climb." Under the leadership of T. Thomas Fortune, the Afro-American League assumed a militantly activist stand. In the formation of the Negro Business League, a program of economic nationalism was institutionalized. In addition, scholars began a scientific defense of the race in studies of black American life.

According to August Meier:

The years following Reconstruction were characterized by an increasing emphasis on economic activity as a factor in solving the race problem. This view was usually part of a larger complex of ideas that included racial solidarity and self-help. It was based on the assumption that by the acquisition of wealth and morality—attained largely by their own efforts—Negroes would gain the respect of white men and thus be accorded their rights as citizens. (Meier, *Negro Thought in America*, 42)

(All noted titles are cited in full in the Bibliography. Titles are included in the notes only to distinguish between several works by a single author.)

2. Novels concerned with moral uplift are *Megda* (1891), *Iola Leroy* (1892), *The Hazeley Family* (1894), *Contending Forces* (1900), *Of One Blood* (1902), *Hope's Highway* (1918), *Black and White Tangled Threads* (1920), and *Kenneth* (1920).

Novels concerned with protest themes included all of the above except *The Hazeley Family*. Novels concerned with race uplift included all of the above except *The Hazeley Family* and *Megda*.

There is no known existing copy of *Who Was Responsible?* (1919).

3. Novels focusing on spiritual uplift, except for *The Hazeley Family* and *Megda*, are devoted also to race uplift and protest. Since moral uplift and protest are primary considerations in these novels and race uplift secondary, uplift and protest are the primary foci of the chap-

ter. Because the novels chosen to illustrate these themes are also concerned with race uplift, this theme is incorporated into the discussion of the novels.

4. Benjamin Quarles identifies two phases of American abolitionism, with Negroes participating more prominently in the latter. The pre–1830 phase was moderate and conciliatory in tone and had a distinctly religious orientation. Though not church centered, new-school abolitionism maintained that gradualism was "wrong in theory, weak in practice, and fatally quieting to the conscience of the slaveholder." Its proponents believed in direct confrontation and in the necessity of overstating their case to make their point. After about 1840, Negroes soberly reappraised the movement and concluded that the Negro must look more closely to his own organizations for support, he must ". . . put into fuller anti-slavery use his own organizations." Quarles, *Black Abolitionists*, 15, 28, 54.

5. Harper, 217–18, 224.

6. Hopkins, *Contending Forces*, 332.

7. Hopkins, "Munroo Rogers," 21.

8. Du Bois, *The Negro in the South*, 172–85.

9. Concern with racial uplift is expressed in *Iola Leroy*, *Hope's Highway*, *Contending Forces*, *Of One Blood*, and *Kenneth*. Race is only a minor theme in *Megda*, and characters in *The Hazeley Family* are probably white.

10. Frederick Douglass attributed post–Reconstruction vilification of Negroes to the threat freedmen posed as potentially equal members of the body politic.

Mark, if you please, the fact . . . that at no time in the history of the conflict between slavery and freedom in this country has the character of the Negro as a man been made the subject of a fiercer and more serious discussion in all the avenues of debate than during the past and present year. Against him have been marshalled the whole artillery of science, philosophy, and history. We are not only confronted by open foes, but we are assailed in the guise of sympathy and friendship and presented as objects of pity. (Brotz, 312)

11. This concern was analogous to that of the antebellum period when evidence of progress and morality among free blacks supposedly lent support to the cause for abolition. black reformers, as well as white, believed it the duty of free Negroes to support the cause of their enslaved brethren by means of their moral behavior. Quarles, *Black Abolitionists*, 91.

Frederick Douglass wrote in 1848: "A change in our political condition would do very little for us without this [character]. Character

is the important thing, and without it we must continue to be marked
for degradation and stamped with the brand of inferiority." (Brotz,
207)

12. An important theme in *Of One Blood, Black and White Tangled Threads*, and *Kenneth*.

13. Miller, 146.

14. Harper, 227.

15. Miller, n.p.

16. Dunham, 22, 135.

17. Harper, 282.

18. Harper, 2.

19. More than any novel of the period, *Iola Leroy* typifies the novelists' concern with the broad social goals of spiritual uplift. In its conception of social and racial issues in terms of Christian principle, the novel looks backward to the moral suasionism of the antebellum era. The race loyalty theme, also given major treatment in the novel, is an early expression of the idea of racial solidarity.

20. Ibid., 256. This passage comes from the Holy Scripture, St. Matthew VIII, v. 20.

21. Ibid., 260.

22. Ibid., 203.

23. Ibid., 235.

24. Ibid., 263.

25. Ibid., 265–66.

26. Ibid., 266.

27. Ibid., 271.

28. Ibid., 259.

29. Ibid., 251–52.

30. In the eyes of Afro-American reformers, drinking and slavery were "twin symbols" of the nation's moral decay. In the chapter entitled "The Users of Adversity," Quarles traces the deep roots of the temperance impulse among Negroes. Beginning in 1788 with the denial of membership by the Free African Society of Philadelphia to anyone with a drinking habit, most organizations aimed at the betterment of black Americans condemned the use of alcohol. Quarles, *Black Abolitionists*, 93–100.

31. Ibid., 250.

32. Harper, 186.

33. Ibid., 255.

34. Hopkins, *Forces*, 271.

35. Ibid., 270.

36. Ibid., 271.

37. A theme in *Black and White Tangled Threads*, *Kenneth*, *Of One Blood*, and *Contending Forces*.

38. Hopkins, *Of One Blood*, 729.

39. The absence of legal protection for Afro-American mistresses and wives of white men, and for their offspring, is discussed in *Iola Leroy* and *Contending Forces*.

40. Plantation school fiction portrays the mulatto as either a tragic figure caught between two worlds or as the evil despoiler of white virtue, a threat to white civilization. At best, the mulatto is depicted therein as a social misfit in whose temperament is found the worst traits of both races.

The moral character of mulattoes is defended in *Black and White Tangled Threads*, *Iola Leroy*, *Contending Forces*, and *Kenneth*.

41. *Contending Forces* is the strongest example of protest fiction in the early period. The element of protest in the novel is sustained and unmitigated. No other novel written by a black female so forthrightly discusses lynching, disfranchisement, and economic oppression in the South. In addition, *Contending Forces* is a forceful example of counterpropaganda. Written in 1900, the novel exemplifies the militant assertiveness of those who defiantly renounced the Tuskegee idea.

42. Hopkins, "Munroe Rogers," 22.

43. Hopkins, *Forces*, 300.

44. Loggins, 325–26.

45. *Colored American Magazine*, November 1902.

46. Hopkins, *Forces*, 232–33.

47. Ibid., 235–36.

48. Ibid., 250.

49. Ibid., 272.

50. Ibid., 124–25.

II

LOOKING WITHIN: RACE CONSCIOUSNESS AND SELF-CRITICISM, 1921–1945

In the years following the close of the First World War, race leaders and intellectuals preached anew the gospel of race pride and racial solidarity. Creative artists caught up in the spirit of what Alain Locke described as the New Negro mood made conscious efforts to create works of art which focused without shame on the black man's heritage and inherent racial character. They hoped in so doing to demonstrate the Negro genius and to contribute works which in the context of the larger culture would be the black American's unique contribution to American civilization. Implicit in this new attitude on the part of black artists was a repudiation of limits imposed by exemplary and prescriptive writing.

Black women novelists were greatly influenced by the cultural nationalism of the New Negro period; yet, contrary to prevailing literary trends, the cultural nationalism of the period served to reinforce in their writing a commitment to the principle of a politically motivated and prescriptive fiction.

Fiction produced by black women between 1921 and 1945 is characterized by its moral seriousness, race-conscious values, and didactic intent. These post–World War I novelists used their stories even more expressly than their predecessors as tools of intraracial self-examination. Like folktales or parables, their stories identify and suggest solutions to serious intraracial issues.

While the novels written between the world wars are concerned with the broad, socioeconomic impact on black Americans of national events such as the First World War or the Great Depression, the novelists did not treat these themes with the same immediacy they accorded more group-centered issues. Instead, they described and assessed black middle-class values, confronted intraracial threats to Afro-American freedom, and continued to advocate the ideal of self-help. Of the inventory of issues and concerns explored in these works, social class, respectability, religious faith and morals, "passing," and intraracial color prejudice are treated most frequently and in the greatest depth.[1] The concern of contemporary black women novelists with middle-class status and values was neither shallow nor frivolous. Most of them continued to view fiction as a tool of racial uplift and, like their predecessors, they were intent on defining the path to racial survival. On the whole, the novels contain less overt protest than in the past. The stories, in focusing on the race itself rather than on the perpetrators of injustice, present more realistic portrayals of Afro-American life. The most striking characteristic of these post–World War I novels, however, is their insistent didacticism. Throughout the period, the novelists' concerns are explicitly set forth, and the prescriptive thrust of the fiction is unrelenting.

Race and Middle-Class Values

With the exception of Zora Neale Hurston and Gertrude Pitts, black women novelists writing between the world wars placed high value on the achievement by black Americans of middle-class status. The novelists believed there was a correspondence between middle-class, ethical behavior and the race's social goals. All but six of the stories written during this period are concerned with the achievement of respectable status within the Afro-American group or with gaining the respect of white people. Stories by Mary Etta Spencer, Lillian Wood, and Jessie Fauset focus on the black middle class and rebut the racial stigma. James Weldon Johnson, in discussing Afro-American art and public opinion, declared that, by their very nature, Jessie Fauset's novels attacked mental attitudes and destroyed the racial stereotype.[2] Another critic saw in one of her novels "the confused but burning will to master the passion of the organized body of lusty American prejudice.[3]

Black women writers of the period were such dedicated sentinels of the race's public image that not until the appearance of Zora Hurston's *Jonah's Gourd Vine* in 1934 did they depict a serious moral lapse in a major character.[4] As the novel *Kenneth* makes evident, the black man's journey from disesteem to simple respect entails the attainment of great knowledge, professional status, a noble bearing and adherence to a chivalric code of honor. Similarly, Bob McComb, the hero in Lillian Wood's *"Let My People Go"* is an unbelievably heroic figure. In *The Resentment*, Mary Etta Spencer focuses on business enterprise and dedicated public service as a means of winning respect.

The self-sacrifice required to achieve great personal ambition is lauded in the novels of this new period, and the novelists characteristically portray the difficult path to achievement as a noble mission. From their point of view, the promulgation of bourgeois values in these stories had the same purpose as did the advancement of Christian and religious principles in the earlier period. If black men and women could become educated and/or wealthy, they could wrest respect from whites and by their example provide encouragement to black people, especially the young. The "let's show them" attitude in *The Resentment* is also prominent in *"Let My People Go,"* a novel that stresses higher education and political leadership as means to advancement.

In *"Let My People Go"* Bob McComb vows to heed the message he receives in a dream. The voice of his mother, who is long since dead, tells him to "Be Somebody." Similar to other success models in stories of this period, Bob's personal success has great significance; it represents a landmark in the struggle of the race to rid itself of an ignominious past and to prove its fitness for social and political equality. Black women novelists sanctioned individual achievement not only because it was in accord with the struggle of the race for the regard of whites but also because it buttressed the difficult intraracial struggle for group self-respect, a struggle frequently discussed in the novels in terms of racial maturity and/or manhood. For these reasons, black women novelists urged, in fact, demanded that black people fight for the very mundane educational and economic opportunities associated with the promise of America: "They [black Americans] were not made to cringe forever before the whites. They were men and should have the rights of men, the respect due to men and the chance of men."[5]

The middle-class families in Jessie Fauset's novels, because they honor personal achievement and middle-class status as unassailable vindicators of the race, instill a consuming ambition in their children. Joel Marshall, the father in Fauset's *There Is Confusion*, is typical of Negro men "obsessed with the idea of a progressing younger generation."[6] His children are to be his contribution to the race. For their part, Joanna and Phillip, Joel's children, come to see in their every deed a thrust or parry in the race battle; for them, personal success, despite the odds against its attainment, becomes crucial to their self-respect. In postponing the conventional outcomes of female maturity—love, marriage, and children—in the interests of her career, Joanna wins her father's approval, encouragement, and financial support.

In *There Is Confusion* and in her other novels, Fauset espouses fidelity to the success ideal and also shows the tremendous personal costs such ambition entails. Unlike Frances Harper, Fauset cautions against the total denial of earthly pleasures and enjoyment for the sake of the race. The young adults in *There Is Confusion* are burdened not only with the need for self-assertion in a professional career but also with the need for exemplary career achievement in order to exonerate the race. The novel dramatizes the conflict inherent in the young adult's effort to reconcile his or her racial responsibility with the simple human need for simplicity, pleasure, and a normal family life. Only after Joanna Marshall achieves her career goal and her talent is widely acclaimed is she free to become a wife.[7] Joanna's brother Phillip at last marries the girl of his choice, but only after he dedicates years of his life to the cause of civil rights. He confesses with great relief: "Do you know as a boy, as a young man, I never consciously let any thought of self come to me? I was always so sure that I was going to strike a blow at this great towering monster [race prejudice]."[8] In *There Is Confusion*, Fauset dramatically portrays the unique maturational conflict confronting young middle-class Afro-Americans, an additional hurdle that extends beyond the struggles of childhood and adolescence and one in which the contending claims of self and race must be brought into balance.

In *The Chinaberry Tree*, Fauset produced a case study of the black middle class—its exclusivity, high moral standards, adherence to social convention, and impeccable taste.[9] The black Americans she portrays are equal to any in moral stature and in the stringency of their observance of middle-class conventions. *The Chinaberry Tree*, like Fauset's other novels, defied the racial stereotype and opposed the fiction being produced by the black cultural nationalists. Zona Gayle writes in the introduction: "It seems strange to affirm as news for many— that there is in America, a great group of Negroes of education and substance who are living lives of genteel interests and pursuits."[10] Fauset carefully elaborates in the novel the conventions, rules of etiquette, and mores of this strata of black society. Without a hint of disapproval, she describes the black bourgeoisie of Redbrook, New Jersey, and notes their clannishness, snobbery, preference for Caucasian facial features, exquisite taste in dress, and straitlaced attitudes.

The novel centers on Laurentine Strange, a beautiful, mulatto seamstress who is the illegitimate daughter of Colonel Holloway and his black mistress, Aunt Sal. In the past, their long relationship had both pleased and scandalized the town. Following Laurentine's birth, the colonel transports a lovely white house all the way from Atlanta to Redbrook for Sal and the child. As years pass, a perfectly formed chinaberry tree flourishes beside the house. The story opens years after the colonel's death as Laurentine discovers that her prospects for making a good marriage are hopelessly compromised by her ambiguous social status. In spite of her beauty, training, good taste, and unblemished reputation, she is unacceptable to the

Redbrook black elite. Laurentine's attempt to achieve respectable social status and thereby to gain entrée into this group, is the conflict of the novel.

Narrative elements in *The Chinaberry Tree*—symbol, characterization, plot, conflict, irony—buttress Fauset's contention that a respectable upper class exists among black Americans and that it is a worthwhile society governed by rules similar to and no less rigorous than those of respectable white society. All the major characters in the story—Laurentine, her cousin Melissa, and Malory Forten—accept without question the values of Redbrook's Negro elite. Both Laurentine and Melissa, while attempting to become part of the respectable inner circle, conform in every respect to its rigid social conventions as is illustrated in Fauset's description of Melissa:

She had the modern young person's scorn for unnecessary formulae, yet her own innate regard for convention made her slightly smug. "Still and all it is nice to be decent. I'm glad my father and mother were married," she thought, unconscious that such an idea had never crossed her mind before. . . .

Serene in her utter respectability, bolstered by a strong sense of rectitude springing from conformity to the merest conventionalities she sallied forth to make life full and joyous for herself and to lay some of its largess in the laps of her aunt and cousin.[11]

Malory, the young man Melissa hopes to marry, belongs to Negro Redbrook's oldest family; his forebears have been residents for generations. He is a strict believer in the values of his class: "[E]ven at his age, twenty, his views were definitely fixed. He believed in the church. . . . He believed in family, in the Republican party, in moderate wealth, a small family, a rather definite place for women. He planned to be an engineer and follow just that profession."[12] Genteel and smug, Malory has the highest regard for the hallmarks of his class—respectability, good family background, good looks, tasteful manners and dress. "Of his own racial group, he belonged to the cream . . . in birth, gentility, decency, Malory believed complacently, no one could surpass him." Conscious of bearing the most coveted name in Negro Redbrook, Malory is exceptionally demanding of the qualities he expects his future wife to possess. Melissa, who lived in obscure poverty before she became Laurentine's houseguest, quails at the prospect of revealing the truth about her background to him. "She knew and he knew that she knew of his belief in class, in position, in integrity."[13] Melissa also understands the importance of having an unsullied background, and like her cousin Laurentine, she only wants to show Redbrook that she is decent and respectable.

When Laurentine contemplates her future as the wife of Phil Hackett, she focuses primarily on her future social position: "With her taste, with her skillful fingers and his money," she muses, "she would be able to show Redbrook what dressing really meant. She would show Mrs. Brown and the wife of Dr. Ismay such perfection as they had never seen."[14]

The dreams Laurentine and Melissa have for the future as the wives of Phil Hackett and Malory Forten do not come to fruition. Each girl blames the other for her rejection. Melissa, unaware of her own less-than-desirable background, feels her association with her illegitimate cousin is the root of Malory's rejection. Laurentine, feeling that Melissa's presence in her home is a social liability, harbors ill feelings for her cousin. Their conflict, like the conflict of the novel, has little to do with character or personality. Each simply views the other as a threat to her social aspirations. When Laurentine and Phil Hackett break their engagement, Laurentine expresses envy of the securely placed Mrs. Ismay:

The encounter with Hackett had shaken her to her depths . . . she wanted to relax, to cease being on the defensive; she wanted, she thought, glancing at the placid brown lady [Mrs. Ismay] beside her, to be serene, gracious, amiable and to be all these things because of the assurance of her place in the world.[15]

With the prospect of marriage to Malory no longer an issue, Melissa comes to recognize her longstanding feelings for Asshur Lane, a kind-hearted, brown-skinned man who is studying to become a farmer. By the end of the story, both Laurentine and Melissa are engaged. By Negro Redbrook's standards, however, Laurentine, in her engagement to a physician, has

the far greater victory. "Every woman wants security, un-
questioned position, good standing," comments Mrs. Ismay.[16]

The basic formulation of *The Chinaberry Tree*, which depicts the heroine moving from uncertain to high status and the
inherent irony of its portrayal of a beautiful, well-bred woman
whose qualities would recommend her to polite society any-
where but who is initially found wanting by an unforgiving
black social class, reveals the high place that the idea of respectability occupies in the hierarchy of this group's values.

The idea of respectability is a powerful theme in all of Fauset's novels. Fauset not only endorsed the superficial dicta of
the black middle class, she condoned its fundamental values,
including its stern sexual morality: "One wasn't 'in' in those
days unless one were eminently respectable,—almost, it might
be said, God fearing."[17] Laurentine is not excluded from polite
society because of her own indiscretions but because of those
of her mother and father.

She was young, she was strong, she was beautiful, she had been in
comparison with the relaxed standards of the day, almost ridicu-
lously careful of her name and fame. In brief, she was the epitome of
all those virtues and restraints which colored men so arrogantly demand in the women they make their wives.[18]

With the advent of her forthcoming marriage, Laurentine
finally overcomes the stigma of her birth. The perfectly sym-
metrical chinaberry tree growing beside Sal's white house is a
symbol of all her daughter has won; the tree is emblematic of
the respectability and worth of the New Jersey town's Negro
elite. Through good marriages, Melissa and Laurentine are
symbolically cleansed of the sins of their parents. In the story's final scene, during a picnic under the chinaberry tree,
Laurentine and Melissa dream of the future and of their ap-
proaching weddings.

Rather like spent swimmers, who had given up the hope of rescue
and then had suddenly met with it, they were sensing with all their
being, the feel of the solid ground beneath their feet, the grateful mo-
notony of the skies above their heads . . . and everywhere about them

the immanence of God. . . . The Chinaberry Tree became a temple.[19]

The social value of chastity is treated in other novels written toward the end of the period. In *After the Storm* by Annie Greene, the heroine's social standing depends as much on her good reputation as upon the fact that she is educated. Nanette's attempt to regain her social status after undergoing the public shame of an out-of-wedlock pregnancy is similar to Laurentine's efforts to secure her social position in *The Chinaberry Tree*. In Odella Wood's *High Ground*, the heroine retains her hard-won niche in society by remaining faithful to a much older husband and relinquishing a loving relationship with a man her own age.

Such renunciations are typical of heroines in novels of this period. Irene Redfield, who belongs to a social set Nella Larsen describes in *Passing* as "quintessential black bourgeoisie," values her middle-class status over all else. In order to preserve her social position as the wife of a physician, she steels herself in order to ignore her husband's affair with one of her friends. If she refuses to acknowledge the relationship, she cannot be expected to divorce or separate from Brian. "It hurt. It hurt like hell. But it didn't matter, if no one knew. If everything could go on as before. If the boys were safe. It did hurt. But it didn't matter."[20] In her anguish, Irene learns what she most cherishes is not love or fidelity, the bond between her and Brian, but the fact that her marriage to him places her in the upper reaches of Negro society. Irene wonders, after deciding to share her husband with Clare, if her drive for economic security and a secure social position has rendered her unfit for some of life's other pleasures, such as wild ecstasy, happiness, and love. "Yet all the while, in spite of her searchings and feelings of frustration, she was aware that, to her, security was the most important and desired thing in life. Not for any of the others, or for all of them would she exchange it."[21]

A countertendency to the novelists' advocacy of middle-class values is evident in novels by Gertrude Pitts and Zora Neale Hurston. Pitts bitterly denounces as shallow and immoral the middle-class values of the younger generation. She claims that

the moral sensibilities of young black people had not been suf-
ficiently developed, because they had been reared by parents
whose greatest hopes were for the empty tokens of middle-class
status. Reactionary in spirit, *Tragedies of Life* reveals the degree to which Pitts deplored black middle-class values and
longed for the more constrained moral choices of a bygone era.
The skull and crossbones adorning its title page serve as a stark
reminder to Negro strivers who, in their haste to acquire material goods and other middle-class attainments, forget to honor
the past and neglect the moral training of their children.

Unlike other black women novelists of the period, Zora Neale
Hurston's consideration of moral conduct was informed by a
scientific, or anthropological, point of view. In several novels,
Hurston examines the moral behavior of Southern black folk
as an index of Afro-American acculturation. She was keenly
interested in the process by which change in the culturally alien, behavioral norms of African Americans could be seen as
a barometer of their will to adapt and survive in a new setting. Because of Hurston's sustained interest in Afro-American folk life, she never received the approval of black middle-
class literary critics.[22] The folk realism which typifies her work
went unappreciated by those who saw the Afro-American novel
as a public relations vehicle that should enhance the racial
image and who argued passionately that portraying the "sordid" elements of Afro-American life should not be countenanced because this reinforced the racial stereotype.[23] Two
years before the appearance of Hurston's *Jonah's Gourd Vine*,
E. Burgum wrote in praise of *The Chinaberry Tree*:

[The novel] shows that Negro life can be complex . . . the ideal of
respectability that dominates the book is more than an adoption of
its stuffy Puritanic survival in the suburban life of bourgeois whites.
For any race that suffers consciously from the surrounding prejudice,
the attainment of respectability is the one sort of imitation that can
eradicate it.[24]

The fictional war to win white respect was still being waged
in the thirties and forties by most black women novelists who,
similar to later proponents of the sixties black Arts move-

ment, sought to constrain artistic expression in the interest of the black American's sociopolitical goals.

The Ideology of Self-Help

The idea of race uplift through self-help had been gaining momentum among Afro-Americans since the end of the Reconstruction era.[25] The self-help impulse found initial expression in the institutional life of the Afro-American community in the black church, in mutual benefit societies, and in the Negro convention movement.[26] The growing acceptance of the self-help idea by black Americans resulted from their virtual exclusion from the institutional life of the white majority before and after slavery, the consequent growth of black institutions, the influence of Booker T. Washington and the general agreement among other black leaders about the need for racial solidarity and self-sufficiency and, finally, from the changes within the class structure of the Afro-American community.[27] Alain Locke noted in *The New Negro* the unmistakable signs of the race pride and optimism previous generations of Afro-American leaders had sought to encourage:

When the race leaders of twenty years ago had spoken of developing race-pride and stimulating race-consciousness, and the desirability of race solidarity, they could not to any accurate degree have anticipated the abrupt feeling that has surged up and now pervades the awakened centers.

Each generation will have its creed, and that of the present is the belief in the efficacy of collective effort, in race co-operation. This deep feeling of race is at present the mainspring of Negro life.[28]

The impact of the self-help idea can be seen in the novelists' treatment of themes of race betterment and leadership. Their idealization of the service concept and their advocacy of racial self-sufficiency constitute a dominant trend in the fiction of the period. The stories portray personal self-sacrifice on behalf of the race as a privilege and moral duty. It is the final step in the individual's quest for self-respect and manhood. None of the stories advocates a radical form of black nationalism.[29] The self-help theme is most frequently explored in terms of the black person's obligation to share a very conventional kind of success with his or her fellows. On the other hand, some stories reveal a strange ambivalence; beneath their surface advocacy of racial self-help one discovers the assumption that white people have a kind of feudal responsibility for black people.[30] This ambivalent attitude is present even in novels written toward the end of the Second World War.[31]

Most of the novels published between the world wars express an ideal of service which obtained in a certain stratum of the black community. The values and lofty ideals of this emergent group were formed, to a great extent, by precepts defined and internalized during the previous generation; the values and ideals of the black middle class sprang from deeper motives than the desire to imitate their white counterparts. These "dark Babbits" needed to plumb far beneath the surface of the American success ethic in order to arrive at tenets of a survival ethic based on the exigencies of color and race.[32] It was a search that involved the testing of many beliefs. In the years after the Reconstruction period, Afro-Americans had been urged by their leaders to solve the problems of race through self-help, moral elevation, industry and hard work, a group economy, the leadership of the talented tenth.[33] We see in these novels written by black women of the period the tenaciousness of the belief in racial self-salvation through the race-conscious dedication of each black individual—the concept of race uplift through service and self-help.

The novels written in the post–World War I period frequently open with expressions of hope that the story presented will be a factor in the struggle for uplift. Annie Nelson's *After the Storm* is dedicated to her mother "whose Christian influence inspired me to live a life of service."[34] Robert Jones wrote in his introduction to *"Let My People Go"*: "Here is a love story in which hero and heroine are dominated by the unselfish motive of service." Mary Spencer, the author of the novel, does not hesitate to comment editorially even within the narrative itself: "Dear readers, if you are striving to convince the slow-awakening race to some idea of purpose, do not tire, if at first they seem unable to grasp your meaning. Ere many years have passed, if not you, others will see the efforts [results?] of your work."[35]

The spirit of asceticism and selflessness being touted in novels written by black women during this era finds its most extreme expression in *Moses, Man of the Mountain* by Zora Neale Hurston.[36] Moses chastises the Israelites at one point in the story: "I had the idea all along you came out here [to the desert] hunting freedom. I didn't know you were hunting a barbecue. Freedom looks like the biggest thing that God ever made to me, and being hungry for the sake of it ought not to stop you."[37]

A young man who had dedicated years of his life to the Negro cause tells his fiancée in Fauset's *There Is Confusion* that he never allowed personal considerations to influence him as a boy; he has been conscious only of the exacting demands of race:

Now as I look back, I think I realize for the first time what this awful business of color in America does to a man. . . . If we weren't so persistently persecuted and harassed that we can think, breathe, do nothing but consider our great obsession, you and I might have been happy long ago. I'd have done as most men of other races do; settled my own life and then launched on some high endeavor.[38]

Phillip is a prototype in *There Is Confusion* of W.E.B. Du Bois who also appears thinly veiled as the eminent race leader in Fauset's *Plum Bun*. Although Van Meier is an advocate of self-help, he urges that beauty and pleasure be introduced deliberately into Negro life, because the struggle for race betterment will require a long period of great self-denial. The racial cause is a unique one, Van Meier says, and those who succeed in attaining higher education and financial success must not then forget to assist their less fortunate brethren.[39]

Zora Neale Hurston argues in *Moses, Man of the Mountain* that the struggle for Afro-American freedom will require unsparing self-sacrifice.[40] This theme is starkly underscored in the novel in a scene that takes place at the end of the Exodus when Moses takes Aaron to the top of the mountain and bids him remove his priestly robes. Moses, explaining to Aaron why

Aaron will not be permitted to enter Canaan and why Aaron's life will not be spared, tells him that the future of Israel is greater than the duty to show pity or mercy for one man. Aaron's life will not be spared because nothing and no one has been spared in the history of Israel's quest for freedom, not the first-born male children, Pharoah, nor Moses himself. Moses asks if in sacrificing Aaron, he is slaying his own brother; he wonders if Aaron, who still loves the old gods, pagan rituals, and dance, the trappings of religious and political power despite his experience and Moses' admonitions, is not Moses himself in other moods.[41] The lesson of Aaron's life and death in the novel is that legitimate claims of the individual must be denied for the cause of freedom.

The novelists' ideas about achieving racial self-determination through collective effort is presented in a number of stories that focus on race leadership. In these stories, a yearning for the advent of a singular personality, a black Moses or a Messiah who will lead the race to freedom, is revealed.[42] Toward the end of the period, this focus shifts to a stress on the leadership role of the black middle class and is seen in the novelists' idealization of service to the race.

While courage, persistence, and selflessness are typical of the race leaders and the success models black women present in the fiction, no leading figure in a novel of the period possesses the moral fortitude and spiritual power of the Moses of Hurston's story. The Moses of *Moses, Man of the Mountain* is a giant and in his character Hurston defines the rigorous constellation of qualities required of those who would lead the race.

Written with sustained narrative power, *Moses, Man of the Mountain* is a lengthy, fictional allegory in which Jews in the Holy Land represent American blacks. The tale, which is marked by the deceptive simplicity of a parable or folktale, falls within the oldest tradition of black folk expression. Its serious theme is well masked by a broadly human, sympathetic, and satirical humor. The colloquial speech of black Americans issues incongruously from the mouths of ancient Jews. The story follows the convention, typical of the Afro-American folktale, of explaining or moralizing by indirection. As in a fable, an aura of mystery surrounds certain characters and events.

Moses' birth and disappearance on Mount Nebo are shrouded in mystery as is his relationship with God which enables him to lead the Jews to freedom. According to Hurston, the tale is her version of a myth that has endured for thousands of years and which exists in infinite variety throughout the world, including Africa. Among American blacks, she says, the myth has special meanings because "wherever children of Africa have been scattered by slavery, there is acceptance of Moses as the fountain of mystic powers." In Africa, Hurston writes in her introduction to the novel, the traditional worship of Moses does not flow from the deliverance of the Ten Commandments on Mount Sinai, but from the mysterious power that enabled him to lead a people to freedom. "It is his rod of power, the terror he showed before all Israel and to Pharoah, and THAT MIGHTY HAND."[43]

In stressing the universality of the Moses myth and pointing to its presence in the imaginative lore of American blacks, Hurston compares the black American's struggle for freedom to similar human struggles throughout history. Because folklore (songs, tales, sayings) arises over time and reflects the collective beliefs and aspirations of unlettered people, Hurston's very use of it as a fictional device in the story implies the universal nature of the desire for freedom as well as the idea that the cultural heritage of a people may succor them spiritually and guide them to freedom.

Another important idea in *Moses, Man of the Mountain* is that beyond the condition of actual enslavement, freedom is an internal matter and must be self-won. Only the story's initial chapters are concerned with the Jews' physical enslavement in Goshen. The rest of the story teaches that the realization of freedom entails a tremendous emotional and spiritual effort for a formerly enslaved people. Physical emancipation must precipitate an intellectual and emotional transformation from dependence to independence, and it is the leader's role to inspire this change. In Moses' character and in the substance of his leadership, Hurston sets forth the requisite qualities and behavior she believed to be necessary in order for Afro-Americans to experience a full measure of freedom. Each lesson in the story is essentially a lesson in racial self-

centeredness and independence. The concept of racial self-help
is expressed within the larger context of a nationalism that is
political, economic, and cultural.

Hurston uses the sojourn in the desert to demonstrate that
the Hebrews are still mentally in thrall to the Egyptians. Despite Pharoah's death in the Red Sea, Moses' task has just begun: to help the Jews overcome their inertia, to prevent their
reenslavement by convincing them to form a nation of their
own. It becomes apparent that the Jews do not have a sufficient basis upon which to live as free men, for they lack the
foundations which will enable them to be a people. Moses tells
them: "It ain't just to get you all out of Egypt, it's to make
something out of you afterwards. That's the main idea . . . if
Pharoah let the Hebrews go peaceably it won't be months before they will be back here ready to serve him again. If I'm to
make a nation of you, you've got to be cut loose forever."[44]
Events that take place after the flight across the Red Sea reveal the Hebrews' disappointing regression to dependency, a
fictional rendering of the recalcitrance of the slave mentality
as they refuse to fight, complain about the hardships (they even
tire of eating manna), and resume the worship of false gods.
The Hebrews' worst fault is their passivity; they refuse to seize
control of their lives and remain determined to rely instead on
Moses or God to sustain them. Moses hopes their arrival at
Sinai will make a difference. "Maybe there, they would realize
that they were really free people at last. Now they acted like
they knew they were free by ear but they couldn't conceive of
it. They did not believe they could take on any responsibility
for themselves at all."[45]

When Moses finally succeeds at helping the Jews ready
themselves for self-determination, he gladly yields all his power
to the Levites. The Hebrews have paid the cost of freedom in
terms of psychic change and struggle, transformations made
possible by divine favor and by the ignition of spiritual elements in their culture. Arrival at Sinai, where Moses receives
the Commandments, symbolizes the readiness of the Jews for
self-government.

Now men could be free because they could govern themselves. They
had something of the essence of divinity expressed in order. They had

the chart and compass of behavior. They need not stumble into blind ways and injure themselves. This was bigger than Israel itself.[46]

Ironically, during Moses' absence on the mountain, the people fall prey to old habits and succumb to debauchery and pay homage once again to pagan idols. "Egypt against Sinai," Hurston wrote. "It was going to be a hard struggle."[47]

The journey of the Jews to Canaan in the story corresponds thematically to the passage of Afro-Americans from slavery to a still incomplete freedom. The dramatic thrust of the tale suggests Hurston's absolute confidence in the Afro-American's eventual attainment of freedom. In addition, Hurston contends in the Moses tale that universal law governs the process which is inexorably set into motion when oppressed people look, at last, to themselves and to their own resources to make their way in the world. The story's closing passage captures Hurston's optimistic prophecy about the future of black America. Moses, preparing his tomb on Mount Nebo, sums up his achievement and that of the Hebrews:

The sounds of Israel's existence came up to him. . . . Moses felt happy over that. His dreams had in no way been completely fulfilled. He had meant to make a perfect people, free and just, noble and strong, that should be a light for all the world and for time and eternity. . . . He had found out that no man may make another free. Freedom was something internal. . . . All you could do was to give the opportunity for freedom and the man himself must make his own emancipation. . . . Israel was at the Jordan inside as well as out. Perhaps he had done as much as possible for one man to do for another. . . . He had given Israel the notes to songs. The words would be according to their own dreams, but they could sing.

They might not be absolutely free inside, but anyway he had taken from them the sorrow of serving without will, and given them the strife of freedom. He had called to their memories the forgotten words of love and family. They had the blessings of being responsible for their own.[48]

Moses would end in mystery, but the law he brought would stand.

Intraracial Color Bias

The importance of skin color in American life and in Afro-American life evoked a powerful response in the fiction of the period. In numerous instances, black women novelists discuss skin color as a matter separate and distinct from racial identity. The stories unanimously decry the power of skin color to divide black Americans, and in their stories, black women tried to objectify this powerful social reality and to expose its influence, especially within the race itself.[49] Many novels of the period document the many ways in which skin color can be the decisive element in a black man or woman's life.[50]

Hugh Gloster wrote of Angela Murray in Fauset's *Comedy, American Style*: "[In] spite of her mother's dictum, that life is more important than color, Angela comes to realize . . . that her treatment of color is the most important factor in her method of living life."[51] There is a great irony in this story, however, for Fauset presents two contradictory themes: (1) skin color should not be allowed to count so much, and (2) since color is so important, it is best to be as white as possible. This second and subliminal message is inescapably conveyed not only because of Fauset's failure to develop the first theme consistently but, more subtly, through her failure to portray heroes and heroines in the story with dark skin and Negroid facial features.[52]

Other black women novelists treated skin color in the stories to comment on the practice of "passing." While most of the novelists countenanced the act of assuming a white identity temporarily for the sake of convenience, they regarded the more serious and permanent defections of light-skinned Afro-Americans as disloyal and destructive to the racial group. Although opposition to "passing" is the avowed position taken most frequently, in a number of the stories, the novelist's treatment of this theme is marked by curious inconsistencies.[53]

In several of the novels, the theme of "passing" is used to illustrate the disruptive effect of color bias within the black American family. The central incident in Jessie Fauset's *Plum Bun* is the betrayal and abandonment of a dark-skinned young woman by her light-complexioned sister. In *Comedy, Ameri-*

can Style, Fauset unravels an even more poignant rift, the outright rejection of a beautiful but dark-skinned child by his light-skinned mother. Similarly, the major concern in Mercedes Gilbert's *Aunt Sara's Wooden God* is the manner in which color bias poisons family and community relationships. In this tale, the fair skin of an evil son blinds his mother to her son's faults and leads her to favor him at the expense of his more worthy, dark-skinned brother. The novels contain numerous examples in which white skin is identified with freedom and power. Olivia, the mother in *Comedy, American Style*, contemplates her newborn, light-skinned son: "he had, she felt, a look of 'race' by which she meant of course the only race which God, or Nature, for hidden, inscrutable purposes, meant should rule."[54] Images of containment abound, on the other hand, in the novelists' representations of the dark-skinned, black man or woman's world.[55]

Black women novelists, guilty themselves of identifying fair skin with beauty, freedom, and power, nonetheless, unabashedly criticized the adoration of the fair among Afro-Americans. They often compared this unhealthy predilection to a form of idolatry and frequently used imagery conveying the tenor of worship to illustrate the problem.[56]

> She [Mrs. Turner] felt honored by Janie's acquaintance and she quickly forgave and forgot snubs in order to keep it. . . . Once having set up her idols and built altars to them, it was inevitable that she should accept any inconsistency and cruelty from her deity . . . like all other believers [she] had built an altar to the unattainable—Caucasian characteristics for all. . . . Behind her crude worship was a belief that somehow she and others through worship would attain in her paradise—a heaven of straight-haired, thin-lipped, high noseboned white seraphs. The physical impossibility in no way injured faith.
>
> So she didn't cling to Janie Woods the woman. She paid homage to Janie's Caucasian characteristics as such. And when she was with Janie she had a feeling of transmutation . . . and she hated Tea Cake first for his defilement of divinity and next for his telling mockery of her.[57]

Fauset's *Comedy, American Style*, "the most penetrating study of color mania in American fiction" according to Hugh

Gloster, is an extreme example of the overriding concern of black women novelists with skin color. Gloster wrote: "The success of the book as an analysis of psychopathic Aryanism is due largely to the able characterization of Olivia." Possessed by a chill determination to shield herself and her family from their racial predicament, Olivia determines to join the dominant race at all costs. She refuses to be dissuaded by her husband's opposition or her own maternal instincts.

Two chapters in the novel trace the effects of Olivia's obsession on the lives of two of her children, Teresa and Oliver. As a result of her mother's influence, Teresa loses her sense of racial identity; the gradual blurring of her self-image ultimately results in her loss of self-will. During Teresa's childhood, Olivia refuses to allow dark-skinned playmates to enter their home. At the first opportunity, she places Teresa in a private school that has never before admitted blacks or Jews. While at school, Teresa "passes" as white but resolves to give up the charade after graduation. On the eve of her elopement with a decent young man, an enraged Olivia discovers the plan. Teresa, in an attempt to placate her mother, suggests to her brown-skinned fiancée that he pretend to be a Mexican. This incident teaches Teresa that her character as well as her racial identity has been compromised by her upbringing: "At . . . that second when it had all meant so much she had been willing to temporize."[58]

Something had given away within her. Something had betrayed her. . . . That [the scorn of a white friend] was what had done it, that was what had fashioned a breach in the wall which her own instinctive racial loyalty had tried to set up against the ever encroaching sea of her mother's protestations and revolt. And after all the wall had not been strong enough. . . . It had fallen before the first onslaught.[59]

Teresa's loss of self results from Olivia's crazed mothering. When her final attempt at self-assertion fails, she passively accedes to Olivia's wishes. After a brief courtship in France, which Olivia engineers, Teresa agrees to a loveless marriage to a mercenary, narrow-minded Frenchman. Her dark-skinned brother, Oliver, who had always looked to Teresa for refuge from Olivia's hatred, as a result of the marriage despairs of life and commits suicide.

Oliver's sad tale is one of a shunted child who is moved from his own home to that of his grandparents. Oliver never succeeds in awakening his mother's love. Olivia's rejection of him is poignantly depicted in a scene in which she meets Oliver on the street and refuses to acknowledge him as her son: "With the other ladies . . . she turned and faced him, let her eyes, like theirs, rest on his face with a strange and awful lack of recognition. Then she turned away again."[60] Over the years, Oliver responds to his mother's treatment: "Gradually as one who, in order to get rid of a distasteful object, hides it from sight, so Oliver, in sheer self-defense, began to hide from himself the consciousness of his mother's distaste."[61]

The emotional logic of Olivia's rejection is unassailable in spite of its moral horror: "Just as years ago she had felt that Christopher was the sign apparent of her white blood, so now she felt that Oliver was the totality of that black blood which she so despised. . . . To her Oliver meant shame. He meant more than that; he meant the expression of her failure to be truly white."[62]

Juxtaposed with the characterization of Olivia is Fauset's characterization of Phoebe Grant. Phoebe's attitude toward skin color contrasts sharply with Olivia's. When an impoverished neighborhood child, Phoebe is acceptable to Olivia only because she has white skin and blond hair. Although Phoebe "passes" for the sake of her business, she remains within the race by choice. "I like colored people," Phoebe says. "With all our troubles, our hard times, our difficulties like no other . . . they are my folks and I'm sticking with them."[63] Because of her color and her race, Phoebe is rejected by two men in her life, one black and the other white. The wealthy white suitor abandons her when she tells him the truth about her race, and the warm-colored Nicholas ends their long affair suggesting that she marry a white man instead.

In the contrasting nature of the fortunes she metes out to Phoebe and Olivia, Fauset underscores her support of racial loyalty and recommends a reasoned approach to the issue of skin color. Phoebe eventually marries Christopher Cary, another of Olivia's sons, and she, Christopher, and Christopher's father emerge from the Great Depression with their fortunes intact. Olivia, on the other hand, having abandoned her family, pursues her dream of whiteness alone in France. Olivia's doom is foreshadowed in the novel's opening pages in which Fauset depicts Olivia as a young schoolgirl struggling to understand a perplexing Sunday school text: "Behold how great a matter a little fire kindleth."[64] The "little fire" is Olivia's early discovery that black Americans are a hated race, but that she can be easily mistaken for white.

Religious Faith, Morals, and Race

Although black women novelists during this period focused on middle-class values and intraracial issues, religious ideals continued to be an important referent in the fiction. Black women novelists continued to find value in the Afro-American church and in Christianity. Biblical quotations, sermons, prayers, and inspirational moralizing addressed directly to the reader are sprinkled throughout the more crudely written stories.[65] These stories, which stemmed from the novelists' commitment to the philosophy of self-help, stress the relationship between racial uplift and the personal morality of the black individual. Although written to inspire the kind of moral behavior thought necessary to secure the Afro-American's earthly goals, many of the stories imply that only divine intervention will provide the solution to racial issues.[66] In the final analysis, they enjoin black Americans to win freedom by means of religious faith. This idea is first stated in a black woman's novel in Fleming's *Hope's Highway*, published in 1918: "I come back to you my country, which I love and revere. You are unfair to my people; but I believe in your future . . . and I shall believe in you as long as I hear Christ's name among you, for through Supreme Love only may I and my people hope for a greater freedom."[67]

While many black women novelists of the period extolled a simple faith in God and the worth of a humble life,[68] Nella Larsen, author of *Quicksand* and *Passing*, was hostile to the fundamentalist faith of the Afro-American church.[69] Her views contrast sharply with those of Zora Neale Hurston who viewed fundamentalist, black religion as a valuable and genuine embodiment of Afro-American culture. Larsen bitterly denounces the Negro church in *Quicksand* and portrays it as regressive and inimical to Negro freedom. According to Larsen, the black church and fundamentalist religion offered counterfeit freedom as it anesthetized black Americans in order to enable them to endure an "unbearable reality."[70]

To many novelists, however, the black church loomed as an important social institution, especially in the South. In the majority of the novels written during this period, the black church in the South is acknowledged to be the central social institution and the primary locus of black community life. The church is the institution which engages the black community in ritualistic acts of reconciliation. It is here that sinners (temporary outcasts such as gamblers, wanderers, unwed mothers), returned soldiers, educators, and would-be race leaders repair for a hearing, a forum, or a welcome in a communion of the faithful.[71]

Among all the novelists who dealt with the subject, the significance of the Afro-American church and of moral excellence in black American life is explored in greatest depth by Zora Neale Hurston. While religious faith and morals are important concerns in the novels written by black women until the close of the Second World War, Hurston's *Jonah's Gourd Vine* is the only novel to examine thoroughly the cultural meaning of the Afro-American's acceptance of Puritanism. With the exception of her *Moses, Man of the Mountain, Jonah's Gourd Vine* is the only novel written by a black woman that discusses the complex role of the black minister as a race leader and as a spiritual leader of his flock.

Hurston viewed the Afro-American church as the paramount embodiment of Afro-American culture. And because she saw culture as the crucial enabling factor in the quest for freedom, she considered the status of the black church in America a sensitive indicator of Afro-American assimilation and potential for survival. In Hurston's *Moses*, the religion of the ruling class, the Egyptians, constitutes an intellectual danger to the freedom of the Jews. The approved religion in the story is Hoodoo, magic, or the power over nature, given by God to chosen men. Pharoah laughs at it until, convinced by the plagues of its authenticity and power, he permits the Jewish exodus from Goshen. Afro-Americans, like the Jews in the desert, must form a nation to attain their own freedom, Hurston says. Freedom will not result from the black American's thoughtless obliteration of his African heritage in the heedless emulation of ruling-class culture. Freedom will arise from indigenous intellectual and spiritual elements already present in the African-American culture. Hoodoo (African religious beliefs transplanted and transformed on American soil) symbolizes this cultural element in the story. As Hoodoo empowers Moses and the Israelites to leave Goshen (slavery) and build a nation, so motive elements in the Afro-American culture will empower Afro-Americans to win their freedom in America. This power, arising out of culture, is a matter of spirit and of law.[72] The historic moment when Moses receives the Ten Commandments is the very beginning of the Jewish nation. "They had something of divinity expressed in order. They had the chart and compass of behavior."[73] Likewise, cultural elements (ideals and law) essential to nationhood also inhere in the folk culture of Afro-Americans. In 1937, Richard Wright discussed the culture of black America:

There is . . . a culture of the Negro which has been addressed to him alone, a culture which has, for good or ill, helped to clarify his consciousness and create emotional attitudes which are conducive to action. This culture has stemmed mainly from two sources: (1) the Negro church; and (2) the fluid folklore of the Negro people.

It was through the portals of the church that the American Negro first entered the shrine of Western culture. . . . the Negro found that his struggle for religion on the plantation between 1820–60 was nothing short of a struggle for human rights. . . . It remained a relatively progressive struggle until religion began to ameliorate and assuage suffering and denial.[74]

The moral conflict Hurston discusses in *Jonah's Gourd Vine* involves discord between two cultures. Tension in the novel stems from conflict between certain kinds of human expression sanctioned in traditional African cosmology and New World religious ethics, especially the closely restricted sexuality of the Puritan tradition. This problem of cultural assimilation confronting Afro-Americans is explored in the tale of John Pearson, a philandering Negro minister who is, nonetheless, the black community's authentic spiritual leader and its representative before God. John and his flock must resolve the apparent contradiction between his spiritual calling and his human failings, failings which metaphorically represent the partial survival among Afro-Americans of an African ethic. Human sexuality, considered in Africa to be expressive of life force, the expression of Being in man, must now be proscribed as John and his flock yield to a new, and Puritan, discipline.[75] "There is a definite culturally determined value system at work here," wrote Hurston in the novel's introduction.[76] The hold of the flesh on the preacher and the persistence of the practice of Hoodoo by his flock signify the tenacity of African culture in the lives of Southern blacks. African traditions survive in new forms among these folk; yet, if they themselves are to survive in the American setting, they must achieve a state of harmony between their African ethical heritage and the prevailing ethical heritage of Puritanism. In this process, the Afro-American minister and the Afro-American church, engaged as they are with conflicting values, are important symbols.

Hurston carefully established the African cultural background of black Americans in the novel. The tale is confined to a small, rural community of black Americans living in the deep South during the period just after Emancipation and immediately following the First World War. Hurston depicts the war as a momentous demarcation, the second great influence, after Western religion, upon the folk-consciousness of the African American. Beneath the surface, these folk are essentially African. African survivals at the core of folk life are apparent in ritual and customs which include the practice of Hoodoo, harvest celebrations, and the ritualistic use of the talking drums.[77] The celebration that takes place at the end of the cotton-picking season is portrayed as an authentic African expression, although it involves Africans of disparate tribes and regions. ("Ibo tune corrupted with Nango. Congo

Gods talking in Alabama.") The symbol of Africa is the drum
whose rhythm lives within African people. "Hey you dare, us
ain't no white folks! Put down dat fiddle: Us don't want no fid-
dles, neither no guitars, neither no banjoes. Less clap!"[78]

So they danced. They called for the instrument that they had brought
to America in their skins—the drum—and they played upon it. . . .
They tore away his clothes that Cuffy might bring nothing away, but
Cuffy seized his drum and hid it in his skin under the skull bones. . . .
So he laughed with cunning and said, "I, who am borne away to become an orphan, carry my parents with me. For *Rhythm* is she not
my mother and Drama is her man.[79]

The Christianity of the black folk, a thin veneer overlaying
traditional belief, exists alongside a deeper Hoodoo faith. "One
night at altar-call, John sang 'barbaric poetry' to his 'Wonder-
workin' God. . . . He rolled his African drum up to the altar
and called his Congo Gods by Christian names."[80]

Having established the alien, non-Christian culture of the
former slaves, Hurston symbolizes their predicament, their need
to adjust in America, in John's struggle to be both spiritual
leader and man. John wants to express his full humanity in a
culture that demands mortification of the flesh, especially in
sexual matters, for the sake of the soul. The novel's many allusions to God the Savior, God made flesh, reinforce the sense
of John's predicament. John's parentage, like that of Jesus
Christ, is never clear. Resented by his stepfather, John differs
in undefined ways from the rest of the children. His followers
never understand him and eventually betray him. He dies in
the end. Trying to explain his struggle to his uncomprehend-
ing congregation, John asks that the members see him as God's
true representative and also as a man like any other when he
is not performing his priestly function.

Y'all been looking at me fuh eight years now, but look lak some uh
y'all been looking on me wid unseein' eye. When Ah speak tuh yuh
from dis pulpit, dat ain't me talkin', dat de voice uh God speakin' thru
me. When de voice is Thew, Ah jus' uhnother one uh God's crumblin'
clods. Dere's seben younguns at mah house and Ah could line 'em all

up in de courthouse and swear tuh eve'one of 'em, Ahm uh natchel man but look lak some uh y'all is dumb tuh de fack.[81]

A failure at making his full humanity acceptable to the church, John leaves the ministry. In a magnificent departing sermon, he tells a parable in which he compares himself and his predicament with that of Jesus Christ; he tells the congregation of Jesus' miracles, his betrayal and death, and his final glory.

I see Jesus
Leaving heben will [sic] all of His grandeur
Dis-robin' Hisself of His matchless honor
Yielding up de scepter of revolvin' worlds
Clothing Hisself in de garment of humanity
Coming into de world to rescue His friends.[82]

In Christian thought, Christ, after all, is God made flesh. John wants the church to acknowledge that the flesh, not just the spirit, is holy. But the sexual scandals that surround his name offend his flock; he is disgraced and abandoned by his wife and friends at a public divorce trial. His suffering and betrayal, however, certify him as a divine emissary. "If he rides upon the silver-harnessed donkey, let us cry hosanna," writes Hurston. "If he weeps in compassion, let us lynch."[83]

John's struggle to subdue his sexual nature lasts until his untimely death. Although toward the end of his life he comes to prefer sexual fidelity to one woman, he is still chagrined by occasional failure. Dynamically involved with life's problems, John achieves change and compromise but finds no ultimate solutions. The essential tensions of his life are ended by death, but he has done well. In the funeral scene, Hurston succeeds in conveying a sense of the harmony toward which John and the community have been striving. Using the figure of the drum, its rhythm suggesting the dynamic character of life and the essential rightness of life's struggle, Hurston ends (for John), yet sustains (for black America), the tension of the tale. The drum's message is that the essence of life is struggle. The struggle experienced by Africans on American soil—seen here in the strife between Christian and non-Christian forms—is worthy, for struggle comes of the urge for survival and possesses the dynamic quality of life itself.

They beat upon the O-go-doe, the ancient . . . Not Kata-Kumba, the drum of triumph, that speaks of great ancestors and glorious wars. Not the little drum of kid-skin, for that is to dance with joy and to call to mind birth and creation, but O-go-doe, the voice of Death— that promises nothing, that speaks with tears only and of the past. . . . So at last the preacher wiped his mouth in the final way and said, "He wuz ah man, and nobody knowed 'im but God," and it was ended in rhythm. With the drumming of the feet, and the mournful dance of the heads, in rhythm, it was ended.[84]

Notes

1. As in Chapter I, the themes selected for discussion in Chapter II were arrived at quantitatively. Over half the novels are concerned with the black middle class, racial self-help, color bias among Afro-Americans, and the role of religion in black American life.

The following novels are concerned with the black middle class: *The Resentment* (1921), *There Is Confusion* (1924) *Plum Bun* (1927), *Passing* (1929), *The Chinaberry Tree* (1931), *Comedy, American Style* (1932), *Tragedies of Life* (1939), *After the Storm* (1942), *The Dawn Appears* (1944), *High Ground* (1945). Two novels, *The Resentment* (1921) and *"Let My People Go"* (1921), focus on personal achievement by black Americans as a means of overcoming the racial stigma.

The theme of racial self-sufficiency is dealt with in *The Resentment* (1921), *"Let My People Go"* (1921), *Jonah's Gourd Vine* (1934), and *Moses, Man of the Mountain* (1939). Self-sufficiency is a minor topic in *There Is Confusion*, *Plum Bun*, *The Flaming Sword* (1935), and *High Ground*. Three novels considered in this category argue either consciously or unconsciously for dependence on white benevolence: *Aunt Sara's Wooden God* (1938), *The Dawn Appears*, and *Under the Cottonwood* (1941).

The problem of color is a major concern in *Plum Bun*, *Passing*, *Comedy, American Style*, *The Flaming Sword*, and *Aunt Sara's Wooden God*. It is a minor theme in *There Is Confusion*, *Quicksand*, and *Their Eyes Were Watching God*. The problem is briefly discussed in *Moses, Man of the Mountain*.

Over half the novels are concerned with the relationship of religious faith and morals to the black Americans' social and political goals—a question given major treatment in five novels and discussed less extensively in five others. The novels are: *Jonah's Gourd Vine*, *Moses, Man of the Mountain*, *Tragedies of Life*, *After the Storm*, and *The Dawn Appears*. Less extensive treatment is given in *The Resentment*, "Let My People Go," *Quicksand*, *The Flaming Sword*, and *High Ground*.

Except for those cited, no other theme was explored in depth in more than one novel. Race leadership, education, and the black woman's special burden are treated as minor themes in the stories. See Appendix B for tabulation of major and minor themes.

(All noted titles are cited in full in the Bibliography. Titles are included in notes only to distinguish between several works by a single author.)

2. Johnson, *Harpers*, 776.

3. Braithwaite, *Opportunity*, XII, 27.

4. Although Helga seduces her husband on the first night they meet, this act is a measure of her desperation. Her punishment is not a result of this transgression which is hardly a factor in the plot. In Larsen, *Quicksand*.

5. Spencer, p. 37.

6. Fauset, *There Is Confusion*, 68.

7. Ibid., 271.

8. Ibid., 267.

9. The problem of color bias among American blacks is given its most extended treatment in *Comedy, American Style*. The novel explores in depth aspects of this problem which are merely touched on in other novels. The psychological portrait of Olivia, while extreme, has an authentic ring. Fauset failed, however, in her attempt to mount a serious fictional challenge to intraracial color bias. *Comedy, American Style* is a testimony to her own strong, but unrecognized, distaste for dark skin and typically negroid facial features.

10. Fauset, *The Chinaberry Tree*, vii.

11. Ibid., 22.

12. Ibid., 131.

13. Ibid., 256.

14. Ibid., 35.

15. Ibid., 85.

16. Ibid., 159.

17. Fauset, *Confusion*, 31.

18. Fauset, *The Chinaberry Tree*, 124.

19. Ibid., 340–41.

20. Larsen, *Passing*, 159.

21. Ibid., 178.

22. Like earlier Afro-American critics of Hurston's novels, Darwin Turner faults Hurston for the discrepancy in the facts of her personal life and the transcendent resolution of racial issues in her fiction. Hurston's "contradictory attitudes must be remembered when appraising her fiction," he says. Introduction to Hurston, *Dust Tracks on a Road*.

23. Ford, 98.

24. Burgum, *Opportunity*, x, 88.

25. Thorpe, *The Mind of the Negro*, 163.

26. The Negro conventions of the 1830s marked the beginning of organized political activity among Afro-Americans. A phenomenon of the 1830s, 1840s, and 1850s, these conventions were organized by Northern blacks to discuss issues of concern to the race. Question of African emigration occupied the delegates to the first convention in 1830. In the 1840s, delegates debated the question of moral suasion versus political action as a means for securing the black man's rights. In 1865, Southern blacks called conventions in several states to discuss issues such as fair wages, the education of black children, and discriminatory laws. Bell, *The Journal of Negro History* 42, 247–50; Quarles, *The Negro in the Making of America*, 102–3; Franklin, 306.

27. An excellent discussion of the manner in which Afro-American institutional development reveals attitudes about the self-help philosophy may be found in "The Institutionalization of Self-Help and Racial Solidarity, 1880–1915," Meier, 121–38.

28. Locke, ed., *The New Negro*, 7–8, 11.

29. Explaining why cultural nationalists, leaders of the New Negro Movement, could not be described as radicals, E. Franklin Frazier wrote that these men did not see themselves as members of a homogeneous oppressed class. The chain of slavery that yoked their ancestors had actually been broken. Real distinctions existed within the race, and the education and wealth of many successful black Americans derived from their white connections:

There has come upon the stage a group which represents a nationalistic movement. This movement is divorced from any program of economic reconstruction. It is unlike the Garvey movement in that . . . Garvey united his nationalistic aims with an economic program. This new movement differs from the program of Booker T. Washington, which sought to place the culture of the Negro upon a sound base by making him an efficient industrial worker. . . . It looks askance at the new rising class of black capitalism while it basks in the sun of white capitalism. It enjoys the congenial company of white radicals while shunning association with black radicals. The New Negro movement functions in the third dimension of culture; but so far it knows nothing of the two dimensions—work and wealth. (Calverton, ed., 388)

30. Three novels—Annie Nelson's *The Dawn Appears*; Mercedes Gilbert's *Aunt Sara's Wooden God*; Lillian Wood's *"Let My People Go"*—project the image of powerful white men who fortuitously rescue innocent black men from imprisonment. These rescues show the white benefactor discharging his responsibility as party to a longstanding relationship between black Americans and upper-class white society, a relationship which originated in the institution of slavery and which continues in the sharecropping or tenant-farm arrangement. In these stories, in return for labor and loyalty, tenants receive a modicum of legal and economic protection. This motif appears in Lucy Turner's *The Flaming Sword*, wherein a faithful, well-educated girl becomes a servant in a white home and is rewarded for her honesty; in Katherine Campbell Graham's *Under the Cottonwood*, which traces several generations of two branches (black and white) of the Stearns family; in the characterization of Aunt Ziphilia, an older black woman in *The Dawn Appears*, who applauds the Northern migration of her children but finds her own happiness in returning to the plantation and her humble place as a servant there.

31. Aunt Sara's allegiance to the Gordon family in *Aunt Sara's Wooden God* ensures her own family's economic security, marginal though it be, through the promise of lifelong employment for her son and intermittent emergency handouts and gifts to her family. Fealty ensured not only against want but also against both innocent and malicious miscarriages of justice. When the wrong son is jailed for theft, Sara trusts absolutely that her landlord will obtain his release from prison. Her attitude toward Southern justice is one of fear and awe, and she believes her only recourse is appeal to another awesome power, that of her white protector, whose power, like that of the law, is almost Godlike.

Describing a similar relationship in *The Dawns Appears*, Nelson remarks in the characterization of Ziphilia on the largess of the plantation owners. Focusing on the benevolence and goodwill of Mr. Brown, Nelson fails to perceive the inequity of the system that delivers great power to Brown and so little to the Brown plantation Negroes.

Ambivalence regarding self-help is well illustrated in *The Flaming Sword*. Although it contains a passage which unequivocally advocates a policy of economic independence, in another place, it also states the following:

[For] the more intelligent class of colored working people recognizes the fact
that they are never economically secure as when under the protectorate of
the aristocratic and more kindly element of the South. . . . The white phi-
lanthropist furnishes the Negro a home, a salary, and social protection, and,
in lifelong gratitude the Negro will defend the white man and his family with
his life's blood, if necessary. (96)

Ambivalence regarding racial self-sufficiency is also evident in
Graham's *Under the Cottonwood*, a tale in which aging freedmen recount joyous tales of the brief happiness they knew after emancipation. The heroine of the story, who listens as a child to these tales,
leaves the South and finds happiness. Upon a return visit home, she
is reminded of her debt of gratitude to the white patrons of her family. The story, which is told from her point of view, presents in a positive light, the simple-minded loyalty still paid by her uncle to a well-
off but drunken relative who is white. Despite her lip service to the
idea of racial self-sufficiency, Graham's treatment of the relationship
between the black and white branches of the Stearns family shows
her lack of insight into the true nature of the psychological and economic bonds which still held Southern black tenants in thrall to white
owners of the land.

32. Augusta Jackson, 99.
33. Thorpe, *The Mind*, 162–63.
34. Nelson, *Storm*, n.p.
35. Spencer, 101.
36. Even a cursory look at characters and plots reveals the interest in racial uplift through self-help which extends throughout the period. After becoming a registered nurse, Nett Miller in
The Resentment dedicates ten years of her life to the black poor of
Philadelphia. Her wealthy brother, Silas, builds a hospital for Negro
women in her honor, and both he and his wife engage in social uplift
work. Negro leaders Tom Brinley, in *Hope's Highway* (1918), and Bob
McComb, in *"Let My People Go"* (1921), abandon profitable careers in
the North and return to the South where educated blacks are needed
most. Passages in *Plum Bun* (1927) and *The Flaming Sword* (1935)
show the manner in which the segregated YMCA served as a forum
for the self-help message. In *High Ground* (1945) and *The Dawn Appears* (1944), Odella Wood and Annie Nelson write about Negro fraternal organizations, a very old type of self-help association.
37. Hurston, *Moses*, 252.
38. Fauset, *Confusion*, 266.
39. Ibid., 219.

40. Of the novels written between the wars, *Moses, Man of the Mountain* contains the most fully developed treatment of the self-help idea. Its comedic elements notwithstanding, this parable based on the Exodus story is a profoundly serious consideration of the need for racial self-help. The story is also significant because, of all the novels included in the study, it contains the most direct and well-argued proposal for black nationalism.

41. Hurston, *Moses*, 336.

42. *Hope's Highway* is Sara Fleming's paean to the recently deceased Booker T. Washington. A white father makes a deathbed bequest of land for a Negro school to his mulatto son whom he exhorts to be a leader of his people, a kind of Moses to "safely carry them over the Red Sea to the Promised Land." Eventually Enoch becomes principal of the school, whose graduates become the hope of the South. Enoch's death creates a void in Negro leadership which is filled by Tom Brinley. The experience in which Tom receives the "call" to lead is a heightened religious moment, a communication with God. A similar instance of divine communication is enacted in *"Let My People Go."* McComb's decision to dedicate his life to teaching comes during a vision in which a voice reminds him of the needs of his race while, in the background, a choir sings "Go down Moses. . . . Let my people go."

43. Hurston, *Moses*, 8.

44. Ibid., 185.

45. Ibid., 247–48.

46. Ibid., 285.

47. Ibid., 289.

48. Ibid., 346–47.

49. The racial welfare, the novelists believed, demanded loyalty and cohesion along racial lines. In addition, the social, economic, political, and psychological welfare of the race would be fostered by the race pride being touted during this time. Hence, the novelists condemned color bias. The fomentor of ill feeling against Zipporah, Moses' dark-skinned wife, and the "mixed multitudes" is cursed with leprosy for seven days and is shunned ever after. In *Aunt Sara's Wooden God*, Gilbert depicts dissension among friends aroused by the hero's light skin color, but her story does not focus on the positive aspects of race loyalty. Seeing Afro-Americans engaged in a long battle for racial justice, Fauset disapproved of "passing." Those who did so failed in their obligation to the race, for if all people could see the full range of color and personality among Afro-Americans, the logical contradictions of prejudice would be much more obvious.

50. Themes prominent in Fauset's *Plum Bun* and *Comedy, American Style*, and in Gilbert's *Aunt Sara's Wooden God*.

51. Gloster, 135–36.

52. Although many authors lamented the worship of light skin and white facial characteristics, only one story out of the twenty written by black women novelists during this period contains a convincing description of beauty in a dark-skinned woman. The following passage appears in *Moses, Man of the Mountain*:

Zipporah of the tawny skin. Zipporah of the flowing body. Zipporah of the night-black eyes. Zipporah of the luxuriant, crinkly hair that covered her shoulders like a great ruff of feathers. Zipporah of the full, dark red lips, Zipporah of the warm, brown arms. (Hurston, *Moses*, 133)

53. The objective and sophisticated tone of *Passing* conflicts with the novel's denouement. Although Larsen maintains throughout most of the novel the stance of the objective, clear-eyed reporter, the moralizing inherent in Clare's death comes as a surprise to the reader.

The hero in *The Flaming Sword*, a man who abandons his wife and "passes" in St. Louis, also meets an untimely death. Neither wife nor mother blames him for his desertion. Understanding the irresistible nature of the temptation to pass, Henry's dark-skinned wife believes she "had no right to discuss his merits or demerits. There would be no return, for they were separated by a barrier more final and uncrossable than death . . . the flaming sword of color which guards the citadel of white supremacy." (24) For Henry to resist the chance to be white, his mother feels, is "lack turning one's back and walking away from one's hebbenly happiness and paradise." (102) Although Turner punishes the hero with death at the story's end, the rest of the narrative expresses her belief that the color line is absolute. In a sense, Henry is shown to have a right to the white satisfactions of life, because he is light enough to secure them.

54. Fauset, *Comedy*, 38.

55. Color as a crucial factor in the black person's life may be seen in the writer's use of images of freedom and constraint. In *Plum Bun*, an enthusiastic, pleasure-seeking young girl cares little for the tradition of hard work and sacrifice exemplified in the lives of her parents: "Freedom! That was the note which Angela heard oftenest in the melody of living which was to be hers. With a wildness that fell just short of unreasonableness she hated restraint." Unimaginable freedom belongs to those whose skin is white. "All the good things are theirs. Not . . . because they were white, but because for the present they had power and the badge of that power was whiteness,

very like the escutcheon of a powerful house." (Fauset, *Plum Bun*, 73, 97)

In the Angela character, Fauset discusses the limitless cultural and intellectual stimulation available to whites. This she contrasts with the physical confinement of Afro-American life and with its proscribed emotional horizons. She shows Afro-American youth deprived of otherwise common feelings of youthful expansion.

Of all the novels of the period, *Quicksand* expresses the strongest, most sustained images of containment. These images of suffocation, imprisonment, and entrapment are meant, however, to encompass both color and race. Leaving American shores for Denmark, Helga feels like "a released bird." (140) "She did not analyze this contentment . . . she knew it sprang from a sense of freedom, a release from the feeling of smallness." (102) Overcome with dread when faced with her return to American soil: "she was overcome with another [feeling] so actual, so sharp, so horribly painful that forever afterward she preferred to forget it. It was as if she were shut up, boxed up, with hundreds of her race, closed up (120) Helga is ultimately doomed. The quicksand of the title finally engulfs her. A failure at life, her only victory is in her partial recognition of the unconquerable forces before which she meets defeat.

56. "He was her God; next to her religion she worshipped him." (Gilbert, 10)

Dark-skinned ones are barred forever from "that holy of holies" to which only the white are elected. (Fauset, *Comedy*, 146)

Dark skin is nothing short of a curse. Light skin a "fortuitous endowment of the god." (Fauset, *Plum Bun*, 13–14)

57. Hurston, *Their Eyes Were Watching God*, 120.

58. Fauset, *Comedy*, 146.

59. Ibid., 145–46.

60. Ibid., 201.

61. Ibid., 203.

62. Ibid., 205.

63. Ibid., 263.

64. Ibid., 3.

65. Seen in novels by Odella Wood, Spencer, Fleming, Nelson, and Lillian Wood.

66. A fundamental assumption in novels by Fleming, Nelson, and Turner.

67. Fleming, 155.

68. *Aunt Sara's Wooden God* and *The Flaming Sword* reveal the authors' skepticism about the wisdom of goal seeking that endangers

fundamental religious attitudes. Evident in the former story is a concern about the moral risk posed by life in the city which is credited with bringing out the worst of the hero's unstable character. In contrast to the predictable virtue of life in Byron, Macon, Georgia, seemed to hold the certainty of absolute evil. The moral risk makes the wisdom of the hero's educational and economic ventures there highly questionable.

69. Helga's conversion in *Quicksand* ironically signals her final entrapment. It initiates her will-less return to Southern soil as the wife of a fundamentalist preacher.

With the obscuring curtain of religion rent, she was able to look about her and see with shocked eyes this thing she had done to herself. She couldn't, she thought, even blame God for it, now that she knew he didn't exist. . . . The white man's God. And his great love for all people regardless of race! What idiotic nonsense she had allowed herself to believe. How could she, how could anyone have been so deluded? How could ten million black folk credit it daily when before their eyes was enacted its contradiction? (Larsen, *Quicksand*, 290)

70. Ibid., 214.

71. Social aspects of church life are evident in the novels by Nelson, Odella Wood, Fauset, Larsen, and Gilbert.

72. As mentioned above, Hurston stresses the mythic quality of the Moses tale. By combining this mythical tale and the conventions of the Afro-American folktale, she emphasizes its cultural or racial spirit.

73. Hurston, *Moses*, 285.

74. Harris and Williams, eds., *Amistad 2*, 5–6.

75. In the African metaphysic, everything that exists is, in the first place, spirit. In this hierarchy, nonliving things are at the lowest level. The human body is at a midpoint in the upper reaches. In this hierarchy forming one contiguous order, man is an encapsulated spirit. He is not essentially evil and, therefore, not encumbered by the duty to mortify his flesh as in Christian thought. (Abraham, 51–52)

76. Hurston, *Jonah*, 6.

77. Abraham expands the definition of literature in Africa to include oral literature and the language of the talking drum. He explains the place of the drum in African ritual and stresses its function as a highly explicit form of communication. "The talking drums are peculiar to Africa. They were not a means of signalling, but a method of actually talking. The drums tried to produce a voice." (Abraham, 85)

78. Hurston, *Jonah*, 59.

79. Ibid., 60.

80. Ibid., 145–46.

81. Ibid., 197.
82. Ibid., 275.
83. Ibid., 257.
84. Ibid., 312.

III

A HUMANISTIC VISION: RACIAL ISSUES AND UNIVERSAL THEMES, 1946–1965

Novels written by Afro-American women shifted in tone and focus after World War II. The Great Depression, the liberalizing social policies of the Roosevelt era, the international fight against fascism, and the humanitarian sentiment that accompanied the Second World War as well as the growing prominence of integration as an accepted racial policy contributed to a broadening of the novelists' world view.[1] Still centrally concerned with Afro-American freedom, these post–World War II novels emerge, nevertheless, from a much wider perspective. The nationalistic impulse, which had influenced black women's novels in the previous period, was supplanted entirely by integrationist sentiment.[2] The great majority of the novels were no longer professions of the novelists' faith in Christianity, democracy, or the ideology of self-help as solutions to racial issues. Those themes which had dominated the novels after about 1920—the black middle class, racial self-help, intraracial color bias, religious faith and morals—were least in evidence after the war.[3] The stories now focused on the forces which kept the races apart. With a keenness not seen before this postwar period, black women writers began to take stock of large social realities: the complex social, historical, and economic factors that influenced the black situation in America.

With great insight, they produced stories containing analyses of the ghetto, race prejudice, and other social and psychological effects of prejudice and racism.[4]

The novels of the period are also distinguishable from earlier works by their variety, complexity, and focus on the individual. The influence of race consciousness and the straightforward approach to uplift and protest characteristic of earlier periods had resulted in rather simplistic thematic and narrative structures. Racial issues and protest, although still crucial to the novelists' concern and message, are subsumed in a focus on individual character. Rather than using their novels to instill or demonstrate the presence of certain values among black Americans, the novelists looked instead at the effect of racism on the values of the individual. The novelists' growing sophistication as artists is evident in a number of stories in which the resolution of conflict not only carries a universal message about being human but also indicates metaphorically the conditions necessary for the integration of the races.

Racial integration as such, however, receives little explicit discussion in the stories, although early stirrings of the civil rights revolution are presaged in Lucy Daniels' *Caleb, My Son* (1956) and the angry mood of black Americans in the sixties in Mary Vroman's *Esther* (1963).

During this period, black women novelists addressed the special lot of the Afro-American woman with greater frequency and directness. They portrayed black women and young girls with a great deal of sympathy and characterized them as courageous and strong individuals. The black woman's bid for survival they showed being won or lost without society's professed protection of the female and often without the assistance of Afro-American men.[5] A work-driven Rosie in Kristin Hunter's *God Bless the Child* thinks of herself as a mule; she is defeated in her struggle against the ghetto as surely as is Lutie Johnson in Ann Petry's *The Street*. Many of the stories show black American females paying the price of even modest success with an unrelenting physical and psychic effort. Esther's grandmother in *Esther* tells her: "Right now your eyes are shining like electric lights 'cause you done started to be a woman and you don't know the first thing what it means. The

Bible says a woman is a glory; but folks don't give a colored woman no glory, nor much respect. You got to fight for it all the way. Even then you don't get much."[6]

Black women novelists were still vitally concerned with exploring racial issues after the Second World War. In their recourse to broadly humanistic values, however, they now proposed a new rationale for racial justice and an encompassing standard for judging human behavior. In their most successful efforts, they achieved a satisfying blend of protest, didacticism, and art.

Race Prejudice

Over half the novels written after World War II address the issues of prejudice and/or racism. While conceding that the war had been economically beneficial, the novelists expressed dismay at how little it accomplished in ending prejudice and discrimination.[7] Historian John Hope Franklin wrote: "For them the task of keeping the home fires burning involved the elimination of discrimination and maltreatment. For that task was as important as that of protecting the Four Freedoms abroad. . . . At the end of the war most Negroes realized that the struggle to save America's own ideals from destruction had just begun."[8]

Some postwar novels concentrate on racial violence and terrorism, while others focus on discrimination in housing, employment, public accommodations, and services. The great majority of the stories, however, examine the parochialism and narrow-mindedness that underlie these practices, a theme notable in a number of the raceless novels of the period. In Thelma Wamble's *All in the Family*, for example, Wamble uses the Westbrook family's ignorance, fear, and secretiveness regarding sexual matters and serious marital problems as a metaphor for race prejudice. The Westbrooks' eventual recovery from the straits of the Great Depression coincides with their intellectual and emotional liberation. With the onset of the war, they emerge not only from the proscriptions of poverty but also from their limited understanding of human sexuality and narrow-minded racial views.

In Ann Petry's raceless novel, *Country Place*, a World War II veteran comes home to find the provincialism of his hometown unchanged by the war. Smug and malicious, the tiny village still nurses its hatred of the Irish, Negroes, and Jews. Johnny "began to remember all the things he had disliked about the town; but it was not what the driver had said. . . . But the sly satisfied smile that still lingered on his face like a wink, a nudge in the rib."[9] During his absence, Johnny's wife Glory had had an affair with the town lecher, a bull of a man who resembles Mussolini. Glory obligingly greets Johnny in a victory nightgown on his first night home, but he soon discovers that she cannot bear to have him touch her. Johnny's growing disillusionment mirrors that of many of his countrymen: "Victory, yeah, victory. What was victory worth? What did it cost, and whose was it anyway?"[10]

The Narrows in Ann Petry's novel of that name is the Negro section in a small New England town. Yet in a figurative sense, The Narrows is a blighted mental state, the recalcitrant irrationality of race prejudice. The novel is a study of race hatred, which Petry identifies as a universal problem of human society. Its thesis is that the capacity for race hatred is universal and that this reality is readily exploited by greedy and powerful elements in society. The novel explores some of the emotional responses engendered by race prejudice as well as its external expression as racism in society. Petry compares the social dynamics of prejudice to those characteristic of any relationship between a minority and a powerful majority. The novel likens the venality of a local newspaper, which publicizes a nonexistent Negro crime wave, to the self-serving witch hunts of the McCarthy era.

Even the State Department was acting like a harried housewife, searching out the hiding place of mice and cockroaches and bedbugs, any of the vermin that from time to time invade a house . . . looking in every likely place for communists and socialists, for heretics and unbelievers, and uncovering so much dust, so much of what Bullock's maiden aunt, the one with the sharp vulgar tongue, called slut's wool, so much of the dirty traceries of moths, so many cobwebs that the whole country shuddered.[11]

The Narrows' central theme, the notion that race prejudice is universal and not a uniquely American problem, is stressed in allusions drawn from the Bible and from classical drama. In a passage from Shakespeare's *Henry the Fifth*, which appears on the frontispiece of the novel, Fluellen likens the River Wye in England to a strikingly similar river in the north of Greece. He satirically compares the capriciousness of King Henry, who ordered the murder of all prisoners of war, to that of Alexander the Great, who "in his rages, and his furies, and his wraths, and his cholers and his moods . . . did, in his ales and his angers . . . kill his best friend, Cleitus." Fluellen continues:

I tell you, Captain, if you look in the maps of the world, I warrant you shall find, in the comparisons between Macedon and Monmouth, that the situations, look you, is both alike. There is a river in Macedon; and there is also moreover a river at Monmouth; it is called Wye at Monmouth; but it is out of my prains what is the name of the other river; but 'tis all one,'tis alike as my finger is to my fingers, and there is Salmons in both.

> Fluellen,
> King Henry V, Act IV, vii

Ironically, The Narrows is located in the New England township of Monmouth. Its main thoroughfare, Dumble Street (dumb plus stumble?), lies at the heart of the ghetto and terminates at the Wye River dock. Other allusions from classical literature in the novel recall human history and enhance the tragic dimension of the story. Petry's characterization of two minor figures—a brilliant and iconoclastic photographer and Caesar the Writing Man—are deliberate borrowings from classical tragedy. As in Greek drama, Caesar and Jubine function as the chorus and fate. Caesar, whose habit is to scribble prophetic sayings on ghetto sidewalks, is inspired on one occasion by an uncommon sight: a white girl, Camillo Sheffield Treadway, and a black man, Lincoln Williams, walking together along the street. Explaining Caesar's strange behavior to the curious girl, Link tells Camillo that The Narrows' residents take whatever Caesar writes as a kind of admonition.

On this occasion of their first outing together, Caesar's in-
scription reads:

Is there anything whereof it may be said, see, this is new? It hath
been already of old time, which was before us.

                                                              Ecclesiastes 1:10

Just as Caesar's inscriptions foreshadow Link's fate and
comment on its universality, they lend both a static, timeless
quality to the action in the novel. Jubine's photographs have
a similar effect. Works of art, his pictures reveal a sensitive
and sophisticated understanding of the interrelationships of
class, wealth, and race in Monmouth. His photographs are social documents which capture and expose the hidden dynamics revealed in the narrative. These dynamics are psychological, social, economic, and historical. At one point, they intersect
to take the life of Lincoln Williams, whose death is the climax
of the story. Before this moment, however, the unfolding narrative demonstrates the myriad effects of race prejudice in the
small city—in the psyche of the whites, in the personalities of
the blacks, in depictions of the ghetto.

The stream-of-consciousness technique Petry uses lays bare
the psychic effect of prejudice in each major character. Character, plot, and theme are unraveled in their recollections,
thoughts, and unconscious mental states. Petry's use of free
association blurs the line between past and present, obscuring
a sense of forward motion in the novel and highlighting whatever is emotionally salient in the life of each major figure.
Without exception, these important feelings and experiences
are related to race.

In the interior dialogue one perceives the slender outlines
of the plot. When he is only eight years old, Link Williams'
adoptive mother, Abigail Crunch, inadvertently causes the
death of her husband, Link's adoptive father. Believing that
her husband has returned home drunk, Abby leaves him alone
when his life could have been saved by immediate medical attention. In her grief, Abby forgets about Link for so long a time
that he runs away and is taken in by Bill Hod, owner of the
Last Chance Saloon. As the story opens, Link has returned

home from college and a stint in the navy. By accident, he meets Camillo Treadway, a beautiful woman and an heir to Monmouth's largest fortune. Their love affair is to seal his death.

Black people in the novel, while representative, are not stereotypes. Their actions arise from character as well as the the stock situation. Abby represents the prim, middle-class female of the older generation. Proper, naive, and narrow-minded, she is unconsciously consumed by self-loathing and shame. Her considerable pride rests in not possessing traits, which seem to her as faults, typical of the race. She is haunted by the fateful night when, fearful that in her husband's drunkenness, he would soil her rug, she angrily spread newspapers around his chair. The negative repressive influence she is on her son Link is clear:

She said colored people (sometimes she just said The Race) had to be cleaner, smarter, thriftier, more ambitious than white people, so that white people would like colored people. The way she explained it made him feel as though he were carrying The Race around with him all the time. At that moment The Race sat astride his shoulders, a weight so great that his back bent under it.[12]

. . . He was responsible for all other members of The Race even though he did not know them; and he never knew whether he was doing something because he, Link, wanted to do it; or whether he was doing something because of the undesirable color of his skin, and that meant he had no control over what he did—it just happened.[13]

The sense of self-worth and self-confidence that Link finally attains are nurtured by Hod, a hardened ghetto survivor. With the help of Weak Knees, the cook, Bill provides Link with a stern, sometimes cruel, but loving fathering. Weak Knees and Bill teach Link what he could never have learned from Abby: common sense, a feeling of manliness, and a legitimate pride of race:

They had balanced that other world, the world of starched doilies and what will people think, the world of white bedspreads and pillow shams and behavior governed by what the Race did or did not do.[14]

Yet Link's seeming triumph over the potential harm that race could mean to his personality proves insignificant against the odds of prejudice in the world. Coupled with his small personal victory and Abby's own transformation are the more palpable elements of determinism in the story.

Although portentous environmental symbols are established at the outset, catastrophe becomes ever more certain as the story unfolds. A tree on Dumble Street called The Hangman, Bill Hod's Last Chance Saloon, and a pervasive aura of darkness in The Narrows are central to action and theme in the novel and account for much of its impact. The Narrows itself is symbolic of all ghettos not only in the present but throughout human history.

Link, like Jubine, appreciates the meaning of race in America. Having graduated with a history degree from Dartmouth, he is working on a history of black Americans. Yet, neither he nor the other characters in Petry's story can fully comprehend the situation that leads inevitably to his death. Link's death is part of a logical scheme whose total configuration only the reader can see.

When Link discovers Camillo's real name, her wealth, and the fact that she is married, he is overcome by anger, shame, and grief. What he knows intellectually about the traditional roles of blacks during and after slavery overshadows the reality of the love he and Camillo share. The greater weight of historical reality forces him to believe he has simply become the property of a white woman rich enough to afford him: "Part of his mind parroted, I bid two hundred; look at his teeth. . . . Look at his muscle, look at his back."[15]

Race becomes the paramount factor in the relationship, and both Link and Camillo begin to react to it involuntarily. Camillo becomes convinced that Link, who is only trying to find a way to salvage his self-respect, actually intends to leave her; and, with horrible automaticity, she accuses him of rape.

She screamed suddenly. He looked at her in astonishment, not believing that the full bodied sound, born of terror, came from her throat unrehearsed, that it had always been there in the throat, emerging when needed.[16]

Upon Camillo's accusation, the interracial situation assumes its classic shape. At all costs, Camillo's honor must be upheld by the white community, and Link must pay with his life for the uncommitted crime of rape. The narrative gathers momentum as forces inevitably converge to accomplish this deed, the tale itself a mere elaboration of the central message of Jubine's photographs and the profound truths contained in Caesar's scribblings. These truths concern the intractability of race prejudice, and the message of this particular tale is the economic, social, and emotional stake a powerful majority has in the preservation of distinctions based on social class, wealth, and race.

The local newspaper, for example, dishonors its mission by conducting a spurious and racist campaign against black crime that indirectly prepares the community for a lynching. Unhinged by futile efforts to save her daughter's reputation, Camillo's mother engineers Link's kidnapping and hopes to force him to sign a confession at the Treadway mansion.

The murder scene is highly stylized. Link's executioners behave as though possessed—like automatons. Having expected to confront a dull-witted brute, they find it incomprehensible to be faced with an intelligent black man. It is an affront to their preconceptions that impels them, in the person of Captain Sheffield, slowly to take aim at Link and shoot. Mrs. Treadway, already distraught, truly believes the version of the killing she gives to the police.

We were helping the law. Camillo was going to pieces, and we had to do something. We didn't mean to harm the Negro. We thought if he confessed it would put a stop to those terrible stories about Camillo. Then when the Negro confessed [Link told them that he and Camillo were in love] Benny seemed to go out of his mind, and he shot him.[17]

Unlike Link's murderers, Abby recognizes her own culpability and that of everyone who knew him. Even she hated Camillo because of her race: "It was all of us, in one way or another, we all had a hand in it, we all reacted violently to those two people, to Link and that girl, because he was colored and she was white."[18] In this rare moment of insight, Abby real-

izes that Bill Hod will seek revenge. Hod "would never permit
that girl with the blond hair to stay alive, unscathed, in the
same world in which he lived."[19]

Realizing that she is exposing herself to ridicule, Abby risks
her pride for the first time in her life. "She no longer cared
what people thought, or what they said, she, who all her life
had been governed by the fear of other people's thoughts, had
acquired an armor of indifference."[20] But Abby's personal victory, like Link's, is hardly significant. It goes counter to the
thrust of the novel, which states emphatically that race prejudice is an implacable and universal force in the world.

The Ghetto

The novelists' concern with the realities of the urban life of
the black masses is further evidence of their heightened social
consciousness. Not only do the novels portray the harshness
of the ghetto environment but also the nature of those exploitative relationships responsible for the ghetto's existence. These
novels reveal a much more sophisticated and realistic approach to protest fiction than those which proffered a seem-
ingly endless parade of bloodless, middle-class heroines. In over
a third of the stories written after the Second World War, the
urban ghetto in all its ugliness is a recurring theme.[21]

In this postwar literature, the institutions of the larger society, however respectable their public character, are shown
to maintain a cruelly exploitative relationship with the ghetto.
A street-wise Rosie in Hunter's *God Bless the Child* is stunned
to learn that the apex of the underworld is located outside the
ghetto. The enigmatic and shadowy figure she thought was a
Mafia kingpin answers to an even more powerful figure on the
outside. "The idea that The Man might have a Man of his own
was upsetting, like stumbling into a hall of mirrors."[22] Lutie
Johnson, in Petry's *The Street*, struggles along valiantly without benefit of the street-wise Rosie's insight. Unaware of their
existence, she is unable to confront the men and institutions
that influence her life. The note of fatalism in these stories de-
rives from a sense of the unequal and hopeless nature of the
struggle in which the major figures are engaged, a struggle that

involves women at odds not only with life in the ghetto but also with ultimate sources of power in society of which they are totally ignorant.

The stories reveal a special sympathy for black women trapped in the slums. The message is clear in *The Street*: A black woman, for all her decency, stamina, and drive, will lose her bid to succeed in the ghetto. David Littlejohn, one of black fiction's harshest critics, was moved by Petry's empathy with Lutie Johnson and other characters in *The Street*: "[It is] the author's reaching, selfless sympathy that makes the case, a sympathy that allows her to become each character, however vile, each object, in turn."[23] A white girl, Angel Mink, from the novel of the same name, is another example of the sympathy accorded women in the slums. Angel makes a successful escape from the ghetto but only with great effort and the sympathetic assistance of community agencies and a legacy from her father. *Scandal at Daybreak* by Elizabeth Wallace is a "beautiful mulatto" story in which a young mother rids herself of an unambitious husband, a World War II GI, in order to achieve a middle-class life for herself and her children. Although she nearly becomes a prostitute in the process, there is no hint of moral condemnation in the story.

BrownGirl, Brownstones by Paule Marshall is unique among the postwar tales of ghetto life.[24] In this story, the ghetto is depicted as an extremely harsh but not invincible environment. It is, in fact, the natural starting point for those at the bottom of the socioeconomic ladder in modern America to begin their ascent. The novel stresses, however, the immense determination and tragic sacrifices that securing such a foothold entails. The story displays unblanched conflict between those capable of and willing to make such sacrifices and those who cannot.

The method of the story is to show the course of this struggle within one West Indian family. The novel opens in 1939, nineteen years after Deighton and Silla Boyce have immigrated to the United States as young newlyweds. Irreconcilable differences in their personalities and personal goals produce much unhappiness and inevitable conflict, and as their nine-year-old daughter Selina grows up, she must resolve the inner conflict she feels because of the opposing ideals of her parents. Selina is caught between the idyllic romanticism of her father and the tough-minded materialism of her mother. Deighton dreams of returning to a small parcel of land in Barbados, while Silla is determined to achieve an economic foothold in America. Deighton's dreams are just that—dreams; they require nothing and he does nothing to make them a reality. Silla's dreams, however, are very real and she gives them the soul-killing effort they require, aided by her friends and other like-minded West Indians in the Brooklyn ghetto.

The struggle between Deighton and Silla centers on Silla's determination to own their own brownstone. In the end, the romantic and impractical Deighton is vanquished by his wife who is a terrifying pillar of determination and strength. Silla symbolizes the spirit of endurance and survival, while Deighton, a most attractive figure at the beginning of the narrative, comes to represent the very essence of defeat.

In the chapter, entitled "The War," Deighton and Silla quarrel over the purchase of the brownstone. Having spent years in America as a day worker, Silla wants Deighton to sell a bequest of land in order to make the down payment on their home. The unrealistic Deighton, who has begun and then abandoned numerous other schemes, wants to return to Barbados, start a small business, and build a fabulous home on less than two acres of land. Tensions mount as Deighton refuses to sell the property or to discuss his plans. When Silla can bear no more, she secretly sells the land after spending months learning to forge her husband's signature. Steadfast before Deighton's horror at the loss of his dream, Silla cries remorselessly, "Yes, Silla has done it. She has lied and feigned and forged. She has damned her soul but she did it."

Selina is horrified at her mother's deed; yet, as she grows older, she begins to realize that Silla's determination is typical of other West Indians in Brooklyn, especially the women. Theirs is a determination that casts the Deightons of the world aside. Although their material gains are small, the costs are monumentally high in terms of self-sacrifice and cruelty. Primarily interested in the house, Silla even sacrifices aspects of her sexuality. At one point, she steels herself to bear Deighton's infidelity: "Suddenly she felt old and barren, deprived, outside the circle of life. But she only succumbed briefly to this feeling, then her back was stiff again, her face resolute, and she sucked her teeth, dismissing them all."[25]

The philosophy of other progressive island immigrants finds expression in the activities of The West Indian Homeowners and Businessman's Association. At one of their meetings, Selina overhears the mothers discuss their roomers. When Iris, a friend of Silla's, expresses sympathy for the unlucky tenants, she is quickly cut down. Florrie's "enraged whisper cleaves Iris' voice."

Sorry for roomers? Sorry? But Gor-blind yah, Iris, who did sorry for you? I ain sorry for a blast. I had to get mine too hard. Let the roomers get out and struggle like I did. I sorry for all the long years I din have nothing and my children din have and now I got little something I too fat and old to enjoy it and my only son dead in those people bloody war and he can't enjoy it. That's what I sorry for![26]

And though her tone is soft, Silla's statement of agreement is the declaration of all she has lived for and believed in.

People got to make their own way. And nearly always to make your way in this Christ world you got to be hard and sometimes misuse others, even your own. Oh, nobody wun admit it. We don talk about it, but we does live by it—each in his own way.[27]

When Deighton, in turn, tricks Silla out of the money from the land sale, she goes to a loan shark, makes the down payment for the house, and fills it with roomers. She tells Deighton: "I wun make mistakes this time. . . . Nothing, nothing gon stop me. I gon steel my heart and bide my time and see you dead—dead at my feet!"[28]

Ironically, Deighton is glad to be free of his dream. His many schemes are a terrible burden, the necessary preface to a final and full acceptance of defeat: "It was as though Silla, by selling the land, had unwittingly spared him the terrible onus of wresting a place in life. The pretense was over. He was broken, stripped, but delivered."[29] Sometime later, after a factory accident, Deighton loses the use of his arm. Welcoming this further attenuation of his manhood, he ignores the therapy that can lead to a partial recovery. As weak as Silla is courageous, he retreats even further from reality into the sanctuary of religious belief; he leaves home completely and goes to live in the house of Father Peace (Father Divine?).

Selina cannot coax her father from the house of Father Peace, but in her wrath, Silla succeeds. Ashamed of losing her husband to this religious dream world, Silla informs the authorities of his status as an illegal alien knowing that Deighton will be deported. Before his departure, she angrily pleads that he acknowledge the reality of America's promise. She demands that he see what she herself understands: the promise of America is a material one, that the country feeds on and yet rewards those who are practical and strong; it annihilates without mercy those who are too weak or too delicate to grub for their dreams.

It's not that I's avaricious or money-mad. . . . Or that I's a follow-pattern so that everything they do I must do. But c'dear, if you got a piece of man you want to see him make out like the rest. You want to improve. Isn't that why people does come to this place? She put the question to his blank stare. . . . You don belong here, mahn.[30]

As the boat comes within sight of Barbados, Deighton leaps over the side.

For months, Selina clings to her grief for her father. Although she realizes that he has failed her, she cannot embrace the crass and narrow-minded world of her mother. Though it holds the promise of belonging and security, she knows that a lifetime among the West Indian strivers will stifle her spiritually.

Two events force Selina to understand, at last, her mother's awesome drive for security. Outside the ghetto for the first time, she has a scalding initiation into the reality of race prejudice while attending college. Out of the pain of this experience, she realizes how thoroughly she has been protected by her mother. For the first time, she understands why Silla grapples with a world that Deighton refused to face. It is a menacing world outside the ghetto that waits to confront Selina, too, with the full meaning of her blackness.

She was one with Miss Thompson. . . . One with the whores, the flashy men, and the blues rising sacredly above the plain of neon lights and ruined houses. . . . And she was one with them: the mother and the Bajan women, who had lived each day what she had come to know. How had the mother endured, she who had not chosen death by water?[31]

Selina realizes that she is encircled and protected by the ghetto. Among the West Indians in Brooklyn, she knows belonging and warmth. This enclave, a ghetto within a ghetto, holds for its children the promise of a future, and this promise is the achievement of her mother's generation.

Selina is at last able to understand her mother's ambition, and the ghetto's promise of protection of its own, all positive qualities. However, like her mother, Selina's character and determination to be free is unquenchable, and she refuses to be contained. The conflict generated by these insights, however, is expressed in recurring dreams of being chased:

he came, huge, silent, swift—a low-slung, dark-furred animal with eyes as innocent as a child's. She could hear his deep growl and feel his breath on her legs. And there was something appealing in that warm breath. Some perverse part of her suddenly wanted surrender more than escape, and thought with pleasure of the claws ripping the last breath from her throat.[32]

Silla comes to represent not only a certain limited approach to life but also the protective and nurturing aspects of the ghetto. Silla and the striving West Indians, represented by The West Indian Homeowners and Businessmen's Association, are one. Nevertheless, Selina realizes she must leave if she is to grow and mature. Now her rejection of Silla is based neither on ignorance nor contempt.

Selina is to receive a scholarship from the West Indian Homeowners and Businessmen's Association. It is an honor she has worked hard to win but which she now knows she cannot accept. In what is supposed to be her acceptance speech, Selina acknowledges and returns the community's love but declines the award, not because she does not deserve it but because it will obligate her to live a life she cannot accept: "The words rang hollow throughout the hall as she hurried down the platform and through the perplexed and unforgiving silence. The loud rustle of her gown, the staccato tap of her heels in the stiff silence bespoke her final alienation. And as the familiar faces fell away behind her she was aware of the loneliness coiled fast around her freedom." [33]

Selina's speech, a fearless declaration of independence and freedom, signals the end of her conflict with Silla. Recognizing in her daughter a more youthful reflection of her own courage and determination, the indomitable Silla relents. Silla sees in Selina the self-same desire for freedom that impelled her to leave her own mother and come to America. So Silla blesses Selina's leaving: " 'Girl, do you know what tis out there? How those white people does do yuh?' At her [Selina's] solemn nod, at the sad knowing in her eyes, Silla's head slowly bowed." [34]

BrownGirl, Brownstones opens and closes with similar images. At the beginning of the novel, an angry young Selina shakes her wrists in disgust, having lost her courage when attempting to leap from the topmost front step of her home. The gesture causes the bangles she wears (silver bracelets worn from birth by West Indian girls) to emit a jangling sound. Selina's developing womanhood, a painful maturation, is the novel's controlling metaphor. Before she can test herself against the world, Selina must resolve the conflict caused by her parents' opposing values. Then she must come to terms with the values—narrow and sometimes ruthless, but sustaining—that Silla embodies in the novel. To achieve a larger measure of freedom, she must leave the protection of home. This is the meaning of the novel's final scene. Walking slowly out of Brooklyn, Selina removes one of her bangles and tosses it away. At this moment, the reader becomes aware of the spatial circumscription of the novel's setting. Selina emerges as from a womb from this familiar enclave, prepared to confront the world. Her gesture of independence symbolizes her birth and release:

The project receded and she was again the sole survivor amid the wreakage. And suddenly she turned away, unable to look any longer. . . . She wanted suddenly, to leave something with them. Then she remembered the two silver bangles she had always worn. She pushed up her coat sleeve and stretched one until it passed over her wrist, and without turning, hurled it high over her shoulder. The bangle rose behind her, a bit of silver against the moon, then curved swiftly downward and struck a stone. A frail sound in that utter silence.[35]

Race and Humanistic Values

In the years during and after World War II, black women writers were concerned with values that were race-conscious as well as ultimately humanistic. Their stories focus on individual growth and/or change as well as on the black man or woman's social environment. This broadened point of view led the novelists to undertake more careful explorations of the effect of prejudice and racism on the individual's system of values. The exigencies of personal and racial survival, the novelists concluded, led many black Americans to adopt values that could preclude the fulfillment of other fundamental human needs. This concern of numbers of black woman novelists with the individual as such was a new phenomenon. No longer did they assess human worth or success in terms of material, educational, or social attainment; such judgments now centered on individual character and were made in terms of more fundamental human values.[36] Gwendolyn Brooks' *Maud Martha,* for example, shows that life can have dignity and worth even at the bottom of the social-economic scale. The day-to-day life of a poverty-stricken domestic has its occasions of pride, compassion, courage, and delight. On one occasion, Maude vows never to work again for a callous white woman who has insulted her:

One walked out from that almost perfect wall, . . . spitting at the firing squad. What difference did it make whether the firing squad understood or did not understand the manner of one's retaliation or why one had to retaliate? Why, one was a human being. One wore clean nightgowns. One loved one's baby. One drank cocoa by the fire— or the gas range—come evening, in the wintertime.[37]

Christine Forte's *A View from the Hill* is a raceless novel about the simple courage of Josie, a young woman who is widowed during the First World War and loses her savings in the Great Depression but who still has the capacity to love a deserted and unhappy grandchild. Because of Josie's love, the child's wounds are healed. Similar to *A View from the Hill* and *Maud Martha, Memphis Jackson's Son* by Mary Beechwood stresses humble characters. In the latter story, an unlettered Southern domestic has much to teach her son, who is a doctor, and the progressive white family for whom her own family has worked for many generations.

Scandal at Daybreak by Elizabeth West and *Caleb, My Son* are curious in their nonjudgmental treatment of actions which, ostensibly, are morally wrong. The story of Caleb, a naive and rebellious young man, is of compelling interest. In her characterizations of Caleb and his father Asa, Daniels successfully conveys the essence of generational conflict and the validity of each generation's point of view. While Asa finds self-respect and dignity in merely surviving and providing for his family in the South, his son's sense of self-worth depends upon society's acknowledgment of his equal rights. Caleb seethes with anger when Asa demands that he stop seeing his white girlfriend and that he terminate his association with a group of radical young friends. Caleb "would have done anything—anything at all—just to prove himself master of his own life."[38] In her description of Asa's shooting of Caleb, Daniels makes it clear that Caleb's mother does nothing to prevent the killing and that the black community, although at one with the family in their grief for Caleb's death and for Asa's role in bringing it about, also gives assent. Asa, ruminating over the killing of his son, finds solace in contemplating an unwritten code that sanctions such homocide in uniquely perilous situations:

He [Asa] could remember how—when he was a little boy—it was rumored that Jack White had shot his son. Asa's father had tried to explain it to him. "It was his right, son. . . . It was his duty." At the time and for years afterwards Asa had not agreed with his father. But now when the duty was his own, he realized the full weight and meaning of it.[39]

Dorothy West's *The Living Is Easy* and Kristin Hunter's *God Bless the Child* present heroines whose compulsive pursuit of a single goal excludes consideration of all other human values. Cleo Judson's compulsion to be accepted by Boston's black upper class is reminiscent of Olivia Cary's color mania in Fauset's *Comedy, American Style*. The obsessive efforts of the love-starved Rosie to buy her way and that her family out of the ghetto in Hunter's *God Bless the Child* can be contrasted with the difficult but gradual unfolding of the maturing Selina Boyce in *BrownGirl, Brownstones*.[40]

Rosie's life in *God Bless the Child* resembles that of a highly active, determined rat caught in a maze. The narrative mirrors Rosie's endless and frenetic activity in its ever accelerating pace. The momentum increases until Rosie, burned out from overwork and nearly insane, returns to the ghetto and dies. In a circular fashion, her suicidal drive brings her back to that which she has fled. Like a mad woman, she flees the home on Madison Drive when she realizes that the ghetto has inexorably begun to claim it, too. Rosie is not defeated for lack of effort or courage; the novel testifies to her tenacity and grit. She fails because her values are misplaced. Rosie's ultimate commitment is to material things. A perfect child of the slums, she is denied the luxury of adequate mothering and forced into independence at an early age. Mistakenly believing that her work-hardened mother, Queenie, doesn't love her, she turns for affection to her grandmother, Lourinda Baxter Huggs, whose false values and influence are the indirect cause of her death.

Rosie is the focus of Hunter's story; and, while Rosie and Queenie are well drawn and believable, Hunter's depiction of Lourinda, Rosie's grandmother, is a marvel. Granny is a self-rejecting, malevolent old lady and the prototypical lifelong retainer whose first loyalty is to her "white folks." Lourinda feels a stronger attachment to the children of her employers than she does to her own. She abandons her bedridden daughter, Queenie, to stay at the bedside of a comatose dowager who is unable to recognize her. Having spent years in the service of the Livesey family, she comes to assume their manners, prejudices, political opinions, and tastes, no matter how inappropriate for one of her station and race: "For forty years she's supported Hoover and hated Roosevelt; refused Heinz's and insisted on S. S. Pierce; snubbed the Italian help and bobbed her head to the English ones."[41] Never admitting her actual poverty, Lourinda tries to impose upon her lusty, unsusceptible daughter the genteel habits and attitudes of a child of wealth. And while Queenie always understands the falseness of Lourinda's mothering, this truth is entirely lost on her own daughter, Rosie. As a child Rosie dislikes and disobeys Queenie. She hungrily awaits the weekly return of her Granny who always arrives bearing gifts—small, precious-looking items she has stolen from the Livesey home.

Both the environmental and personal sources of conflict in the story interact synergistically in their effect upon Rosie. Her compulsion to work and spend money fails to lead to advancement or progress. Drowning in debt, she frantically buys and impulsively gives away hundreds of items, some strange and vastly expensive. Her buying habits reflect a similar inability to identify what is worthwhile in her personal life.

At one point, Queenie asks Rosie to reduce her killing work schedule and marry Larnie, a young man who is truly devoted to her. But Rosie, fanatically consumed by her money-making schemes, never considers the greater worth of the love that Larnie offers. Queenie understands the nature of Rosie's troubles and says: "The kind of gold that comes in a paint bottle— that's the kind she goes for, every time. Now real gold ain't that shiny. It's kinda dull. Rosie don't know that yet. But I do."[42]

One pivotal scene reveals the soundness of Queenie's values and instincts and contrasts them with the false, selfish, and delusional values of Granny. In a wryly humorous encounter, a young con man who plans to trick Rosie out of a large sum of money comes to visit. Lourinda is so taken by Tommy Tucker's floridly courteous manner that she is half convinced that he is the rising young businessman he pretends to be. Exuding courtesy, Granny treats him as a serious candidate for her granddaughter's hand in marriage. With apparent innocence, she reminds Rosie, who works at two legitimate jobs in addition to her illegitimate numbers business: "You got a couple of nice positions, you can be a big help to him. . . . He's gonna be a big man someday." Granny is unaware that Tucker is really a conniver who is in the numbers racket with Rosie and that they have already been involved in an unhappy love affair. The more perceptive Queenie, however, stares at Tucker for so long that he is forced to shift positions uncomfortably. " 'Nigger,' she says at last, 'what you want with my little girl?' "[43]

In a chilling act of betrayal, Lourinda then accuses Queenie of jealousy and encourages Rosie to believe in Tucker. Her own wish to believe in the trickster outweighs any concern for her grandchild. For her part, Rosie is less seduced by Tucker than by her own need to believe in and please her grandmother. Yet, Lourinda's approval depends on Rosie's surrender of her sense of reality: " 'Tucker 'n me, are gonna have a lot of money, Granny,' Rosie said suddenly. 'More money 'n you ever seen. He's started investin' for us already.' She raised her chin and looked at Granny fiercely, half asking not to be believed. But the old lady nodded encouragingly."[44]

In a reversal of roles, Rosie becomes the profferer of gifts to her grandmother. The desire to please Lourinda is the deeper reason for her ceaseless efforts to leave the ghetto. However, constant work and the wild spending cannot earn her the aging woman's true affection. Retired and living with Rosie and Queenie, Lourinda has an insatiable greed for the gifts that remind her of her former life in the Livesey home. With naked avarice, she accepts each of Rosie's gifts:

Granny advanced on the table. She picked up the box and deliberately extracted the fabulous fur mules. Squinting against the light, she examined them slowly and critically, picking at the little seams where the soles joined the uppers, poking at the lining with her fingernails, sniffing the leather of the soles and finally, rubbing her fingers over the surface of the fur.

"Real Persian," she said at last. "Real well made, too. For these days."[45]

Even the house on Madison Drive does not satisfy Lourinda. As Rosie becomes more and more desperate, her gifts chart the accelerating speed of her flight from reality. "Suddenly Dolly wished for a sharp knife to cut through the insidiously spreading web of fantasy in which Rosie was caught. It was all the more dangerous because she was able to make it shimmer for others."[46]

Rosie gives Dolly a fur coat and a diamond-studded watch. She buys Queenie a color television set and Lourinda a rare crystal punch bowl which cost more than fifteen hundred dollars. When Granny praises Rosie's taste after she has bought a bed jacket of authentic Belgian lace, Queenie flings the jacket into a corner, angrily protesting Rosie's latest extravagance, and tells Lourinda: "You wouldn't know something real if it hit you between the eyes." Then once again she tries to make Rosie understand what she has known all of her life—that nothing will ever satisfy Lourinda, for Lourinda has an abiding hatred for anyone who is poor and black. She asks Rosie, "ain't you found that out yet? You ain't gonna be good enough till you turn white."[47] Larnie asks Rosie if she is trying to take the place of Granny's white folks.

Another character in the novel, the middle-class mother of Dolly Diaz, manifests a self-hatred similar to Lourinda's. At the Diaz home, "Even the bathroom was as spotless as a plumber's showroom display. The gleaming tiles, the precisely folded towels, the wastebasket that never held so much as a scrap of tissue, all seemed to say: 'Superior beings live here: they are not really dirty.' Or, more accurately: 'They are not really Negroes.' "[48]

Rosie never recognizes that her grandmother's values are worthless or that her false affection originates in self-hate. Having been taught by Lourinda to see value only in material things, she is angry at and contemptuous of her mother. She fails to respond in a womanly fashion to the man who loves her, and most importantly, she drives herself beyond the point of exhaustion until she ruins her health. "As Rosie got skinnier and more hollow-eyed and coughed more, she gradually got used to sleeping less. She had the wiry strength of weeds and other undernourished forms of life, the kind that thrives on starvation and toughens on struggle."[49] Rosie, in fact, internalizes her grandmother's self-hatred, and Lourinda's hidden influence goes unchallenged until Rosie is confronted with a genuine love she cannot evade: "She stared at him [Larnie], baffled. Here it was again, the one thing she couldn't cope with. Love, undeserved, unexplained." Rosie's bagman, a mild-mannered wino, is killed defending her because he refuses to disclose Rosie's whereabouts when she is unable to pay a series of winning bets. For the first time in her life, Rosie reaches out for solace and warmth to someone other than Granny. Consoled by Larnie, she realizes that "her grandmother had begun to die . . . but that she had begun to live."[50]

Yet, Rosie's emotional liberation from Lourinda merely precedes the novel's last tragic reversal. Rosie is too emotionally and physically ill to cope with her discovery that, just as in the ghetto, her beloved home on Madison Drive is infested with roaches and termites. It is a cruel joke that leaves her hysterical. All of Rosie's striving only completes a vicious circle. She is robbed of any reward for her efforts and, in the end, her efforts cost her her life.

Individual Conflict and Racial Integration

In focusing their stories on intrapersonal conflict, black women novelists did not abandon racial themes.[51] In fact, in several of the stories, the formula advanced for the resolution of inner conflict serves as a metaphor for achieving a truly integrated society. In their portrayal of leading figures enmeshed in the difficult process of conflict and change, the novelists make convincing arguments against platitudinous and shallow approaches to racial integration.

A recurring pattern in the stories finds the leading character wrestling with a problem which is resolved through self-understanding and self-acceptance. An outstanding example of this pattern occurs in Gwendolyn Brooks' *Maud Martha*. Maude, who is overshadowed by a beautiful older sister and in later years is not quite loved by her husband, decides to be just herself: "What *she* wanted to donate to the world was a good Maud Martha. That was the offering, the bit of art, that could not come from any other. She would polish and hone that."[52]

Like the characters in *A View from the Hill*, the principal figures in Hurston's *Seraph on the Suwannee* are white. Racial integration and the individual's growth are Hurston's central themes. Arvay Meserve, the story's heroine, is well advanced into middle age before she finally overcomes the habit of self-deception. Lacking in self-confidence, she takes flight when threatened into fits of religious fanaticism. Born into a poor white family, her problems with self-esteem are exacerbated when she marries James Meserve, a handsome, vital man who is descended from the now equally impoverished, old landed gentry. Hurston's characterization of Meserve is a curiosity in this body of fiction. Jim is a fully realized man, far superior to his wife in human qualities and personal achievement.

Jim considers his marriage to Arvay a partnership between equals. Direct, honest, and patient, he tries for years to convince her of his love. But Arvay's problems become the problem of their relationship, and the marriage cannot thrive until she solves them. After a long struggle, Arvay accepts herself and matures. She rids herself of her old cowardly habits and even learns to be brave.

Seraph on the Suwanee is a powerful and realistic story of love and marriage. The story can be read as symbolically depicting the yielding of the old traditional South to the new. Like Jim, the South of the future could be vigorous, economically aggressive, and successful as well as humane. It could accept men on their merits and not rely on a faded tradition to bolster its self-esteem.

In Mary Vroman's *Esther* the expression of long-suppressed feelings of racial hate on the part of the heroine illuminates an unacknowledged issue of racial integration.[53] Recurring themes in *Esther* concern the complexity of human personality and the profound need of all human beings for one another. Both ideas are conveyed in a singularly striking encounter. A young, innocent girl, Esther, is raped by the teenage son of her employer. Years later, she sees her assailant again. The encounter with Princhett, now vice-president of the local bank, focuses solely on Vroman's ideas about the ultimate value of mutual human experience. Even negative contact, Vroman says, joins one human being to another in a mysterious and fundamental way. Esther's lack of bitterness when she sees Princhett amazes her. The experience is one of pure cognition, the simple realization that their lives have touched in the past.

She had seen in him only what she had felt in herself: the acknowledgement of the bond between them, an almost mystical remnant of the mutually degrading experience.
She had, as she sat there, a wildly sacrilegious thought. That God, Himself was blind to the nature of human experiences, and that He used them only for a single, patient, implacable purpose: to attach the human heart as with so many inseverable strings of its own making, one to another, and finally to Himself.[54]

Although she did not invite the assault, in truth, there was an attraction between Esther and her employer's son. Princhett forced her in anger and against her will to relent, but Esther's youth and readiness had also betrayed her. The rape was not a simple matter.

Recognition of her own complexity is Esther's task throughout the novel. She struggles for years to resolve deeply felt but unconscious feelings of anger and racial hatred. Never having lived among whites, she cannot understand the hostility to them which other blacks openly express. "Hating white people was to her much like hating the devil. Something one said on principle, but without conviction, having small actual acquaintance with either."[55] As a teenager just out of high school and waiting to enter college, Esther's decision to work for the Princhetts is something of a lark. Discovering that she is invisible to the white family, Esther believes she can safely observe and evaluate their way of life and behavior from a distance. Even then, she "refused acknowledgement of another feeling—the delicate hurt inflicted by being thought of as nothing. She sensed that in that direction lay a deeper pain."[56]

Personal success as an adult obscures Esther's awareness of this deep-seated pain; for, in spite of her grandmother's death and the birth of her illegitimate daughter, she succeeds at becoming a registered nurse. Because she also succeeds in greatly alleviating the substandard conditions in the segregated ward of Leemouth Hospital, Esther comes to believe that through dedication and willpower, black people can solve all their own problems as a race. But a dying old man tells her one day that this is not so. It is their very insularity that is so dispiriting to black people, he says. Their forced insularity is the reason nurses and other attendants are always fatigued; it is the reason they are negligent and sometimes even cruel to their patients. And white folks, he says, are just as lonesome for black people, too.

The second-class treatment of black patients in the Annex despite her best efforts forces Esther to see the inherent evil of segregation. Yet, she still fails to recognize her own deep hatred of white people. This blindness leads to arguments with her husband Joe, who emphatically states the case for black rage. According to Joe, anger is the only appropriate reaction to racial injustice. Anger is cleansing, he declares; it clears the path for self-love. Moreover, the novel argues, the acknowledgment of such anger by black Americans can, ironically, clear the path for racial reconciliation. Joe vehemently denounces Esther's attempts to shield their children from feeling fear and hatred of whites. Describing her attitude toward this aspect of the rearing of black children as illusory and dangerous, he says scornfully that, in his opinion, she has grown up a black woman in the South without really understanding the meaning of race in Southern society. He insists that all black people feel racial hate to some degree and predicts that someday she herself will have to acknowledge this feeling.

Most of us have learned our lessons well, Esther. We've learned so much fear that we've finally learned to hate. I mean hate from our guts! It's been a long time coming, but there are signs everywhere and I glory to see the day. By the time that child in there is grown he'll glory in his blackness. Esther, hate born of fear is my son's heritage, and his hope of glory. And don't you dare try to fill his head with this nonsense about brotherhood and the white man's basic goodness.[57]

The story's final confrontation and the climax of the novel show Esther's true feelings about white people brought unequivocally to consciousness. Esther and Joe discover Esther's daughter Hope, the child born of the rape long ago, in an innocent embrace with a secret friend, a white boy named David. Esther, prompted by buried memories of the past, reacts instantly. She leaps at the boy and tries to strangle him with her bare hands so intent is she on murdering anyone who would harm her child. Esther's hands, the life-giving hands of a professional nurse, are "obedient to her single, total hatred, squeezing at the white throat, squeezing the life from every, soft, white boy throat."[58]

In Esther's need to recognize and accept her anger, Vroman identifies and underscores the same need among black Americans. All men, however, need to love one another, her novel repeatedly iterates, but in the face of injustice, they must bear the reality of their hatred, too. Vroman's central theme, the universal need of human beings for one another, is stated repeatedly in the novel. Yet, it is the modification of this theme, in her focus on righteous anger, upon which the plot turns and character development depends. This secondary theme, which is developed with such care and expressed so forcefully, is a major qualification of the novel's fundamental statement. Indeed, Vroman's forthright affirmation of anger on the part of American blacks as integral to the process of racial reconciliation sets it apart from other novels of the period. *Esther* is a harbinger of later novels by black Americans and of a widespread cultural phenomenon within the race that culminated in the civil rights revolution of the sixties.

Notes

1. According to Hugh Gloster, the "broadening of literary outlook from a restrictively racial to a broadly human point of view is the tendency which chiefly distinguishes Negro writing of the 1930s from that of earlier years." (All noted titles are cited in full in the Bibliography. Titles are included in the notes only to distinguish between several works by a single author.)

2. "In response to this trend [integration], the post-war novelists were forced to revise their literary goals. If Negroes were at last moving toward full integration, why not point the way by writing integrated novels." (Bone, 156)

3. Only one novel of the period, West's *The Living Is Easy*, is pri-

marily concerned with the black middle class. *Scandal at Daybreak* criticizes the snobbery of middle-class blacks but is more concerned with the heroine's attempt to escape the slums. There is only one "passing" novel and only in the broadest sense can *Aggie* and *Ice Cream from Heaven* be described as self-help novels.

4. As in previous chapters, themes for Chapter III were determined on a quantitative basis. The tabulation of themes for this period reveals that the novelists' concern with race prejudice pervaded novels of the period. It is a major or minor theme in nearly two-thirds of the novels written between 1946 and 1965. After race prejudice, the novelists were most concerned with the ghetto, a concern reflected in ten of the novels. In eight novels the novelists struggled to affirm the worth of the individual. Also in eight novels the resolution of personal conflict serves as a metaphor for racial integration or interracial reconciliation.

Race prejudice is a major theme in *All in the Family*; *The Narrows*; *Country Place*; *Vengeance Is Mine*; *Esther; Queen of Persia*; *The Reign of Terror*; *Killer of the Dream*; *God Bless the Child*; *The Big Lie*; and *Publicans and Sinners*. The theme of race prejudice also appears in these novels as a minor theme: *Black on the Rainbow*; *Maud Martha*; *Strange Sinner*; *Seraph on the Suwanee*; *Memphis Jackson's Son*; *Wasted Travail*; *BrownGirl, Brownstones*; *Wolf Kitty*; and *Like One of the Family*.

The urban ghetto is a concern in *The Street*; *The Narrows*; *Scandal at Daybreak*; *Angel Mink*; *BrownGirl, Brownstones*; *God Bless the Child*; *Wasted Travail*; and *Maud Martha*.

The relationship of race to individual values is considered in *The Living Is Easy*; *Maud Martha*; *Scandal at Daybreak*; *Memphis Jackson's Son*; *BrownGirl, Brownstones*; *The Reign of Terror*; *God Bless the Child*; and *Caleb, My Son*.

In the following novels, the resolution of individual conflict is thematically related to the resolution of racial conflict: *Seraph on the Suwannee*, *The Narrows*, *Memphis Jackson's Son*, and *Esther*. Other novels containing themes of personal reconciliation are: *Maud Martha*, *BrownGirl, Brownstones*, and *A View from the Hill*. In an autobiographical story, *Wasted Travail*, one finds a totally negative acceptance of defeat.

Social stratification, color, education, religion and morals, and the mulatto are each treated as a major theme in one novel. See Appendix A for tabulation of major and minor themes.

5. While most major novels contain female leading characters, the plight of the black woman, as a black woman, is a minor theme of

the period. Specific comments on the black woman's lot or the lot of females in general are found in *Maud Martha*; *Memphis Jackson's Son*; *BrownGirl, Brownstones*; *Esther*; *God Bless the Child*; and *The Living Is Easy*.

6. Vroman, 3.

7. Race prejudice among whites is depicted in many novels, while the effect of prejudice and racism on blacks is stressed in others. In the former group are: *Black on the Rainbow*; *All in the Family*; *Vengeance Is Mine*; *Country Place*; *Esther; Queen of Persia*; *The Reign of Terror*; *Publicans and Sinners*; and *Killer of the Dream*.

A major theme in *The Narrows*, race prejudice is treated more fully and with greater skill than in other novels of the period. Prejudice is exposed as a potent force in the ordering of American society; it is also discussed in terms of its negative and determining effect on human personality. *The Narrows* is unique in its pervasive symbolism: the novel's theme is that American racism can be understood in the light of apparently universal laws which govern relationships between majority and minority groups.

8. Franklin, 600.

9. Petry, *Country Place*, 6.

10. Ibid., 31.

11. Petry, *The Narrows*, 378.

12. Ibid., 138.

13. Ibid., 148.

14. Ibid., 405.

15. Ibid., 280.

16. Ibid., 319.

17. Ibid., 424–25.

18. Ibid., 419.

19. Ibid., 423.

20. Ibid., 414.

21. Most novels of the thirties and forties are concerned with black Americans in small towns and rural areas of the South. None written by a black American before the war deals with lower-class blacks in the North, even though thousands of black Americans left the South for Northern cities in the years during and immediately preceding the First World War.

22. Hunter, 53.

23. Littlejohn, 148.

24. Because several novels written after World War II effectively treat the theme of the urban ghetto, the selection of *BrownGirl, Brownstones* to represent the group was made somewhat arbitrarily.

In addition to the ghetto theme, the novel, in its realistic depiction of positive as well as negative aspects of ghetto existence, typifies the trend toward realism and away from a heavy emphasis on protest in the novels. In *Maud Martha* and *God Bless the Child*, the ghetto resembles a human jungle, but also in these stories, black heroines achieve a measure of personal triumph.

25. Marshall, 96, 40.
26. Ibid., 185.
27. Ibid.
28. Ibid., 111.
29. Ibid., 97.
30. Ibid., 145.
31. Ibid., 240.
32. Ibid., 245.
33. Ibid., 249.
34. Ibid., 252.
35. Ibid., 255.

36. Hurston is the first black woman writer to portray a character who grows or changes in stature in the manner we have come to expect of heroes or heroines in serious fiction. Twice, Janie Starks (*Their Eyes Were Watching God*, 1937) marries for the sake of security. After the death of her second husband, she rejects such choices and runs off with a younger man, a free-spirited, migrant worker who teaches her the meaning of love. Toward the end of the story, Janie is forced to kill Tea Cake. In rescuing her during a flood, he is bitten by a rabid dog. Days later, in a state of madness and extreme thirst, he attacks Janie and she shoots him. In running away with Tea Cake and in shooting him to save herself, Janie acts upon a basic urge to survive. She affirms the worth of her own life and the greater value of self-love over respectability and financial security.

"Lawd!" Phoeby [Janie's best friend who is listening to her tale] breathed out heavily.
"Ah done growed ten feet higher from just listenin' tuh you Janie; Ah ain't satisfied wid mahself no mo."
"Its uh known fact, Phoeby, you got tuh *go* there tuh *know* there. . . . Two things everybody's got tuh do fuh themselves. They got tuh go tuh God and they got tuh find out about livin' fuh theyselves." (Hurston, 158)

37. Brooks, 116.
38. Daniels, 107.
39. Ibid., 116.
40. While *God Bless the Child* protests the murderous conditions

of ghetto life, its theme is the way personal values can be affected by racial oppression. No other novel in the study so forcefully iterates the ultimate futility of worldly success, especially when the values from which it springs are false.

41. Hunter, 5.

42. Ibid., 132.

43. Ibid., 117.

44. Ibid.

45. Ibid., 193.

46. Ibid., 207.

47. Ibid., 250.

48. Ibid., 186.

49. Ibid., 146.

50. Ibid.

51. The most striking examples are: *Maud Martha*, *BrownGirl, Brownstones*, *Seraph on the Suwanee*, and *Esther*.

52. Brooks, 19.

53. Focused on themes of progress and change which are explicated in the growth of the heroine, *Esther* represents one of the major trends in postwar fiction by black American women. In this story, the theme of personal integration serves as a metaphor for racial reconciliation and integration. As an argument for racial integration, the novel is typical of other novels of the period, while, in its affirmation of black rage, it points to those to follow later in the sixties.

54. Vroman, 96.

55. Ibid., 27.

56. Ibid., 44.

57. Ibid., 143–44.

58. Ibid., 150.

IV

PART OF THEIR SELF-RESPECT: THE AFRO-AMERICAN NOVEL AND NOVELS OF THE AMERICAN MAINSTREAM

Novels by black Americans began to appear with some frequency in the latter decades of the nineteenth century during the same period in which the modern American novel emerged. By this time, the Romantic spirit in American letters had waned, and literary pioneers began to explore theories and techniques more in harmony with new ideas about the nature of society and humankind and the revolutionary social changes engendered by the development of modern technology.

The modern American novel, according to literary critics, is concerned with documenting the nation's ever-changing social landscape, and it has sought to interpret the meaning of these changes in terms of their effect on individual, moral responsibility. Among the modern American novel's major preoccupations is the attempt to come to terms with the diminished status of the individual and, therefore, the reduced social responsibility of the individual in the modern age.[1]

The black American novel, however, proceeds from an entirely different point of view. For much of its history, this body of fiction has been animated by a central concern with the racial group. The cataclysmic social changes that ushered in the latter decades of the nineteenth century and led to the development of the modern novel are of much less moment to the black novel's inception than the aggressive racism that characterized the period of its early history. The wellsprings of the early black novel are not in that challenging social upheaval in which modern mainstream fiction is rooted but in the immediate situation then confronting the black American community.

Afro-American novels, unlike serious novels that were produced during the 1880s and 1890s are, until the post–World War I period, romantic and idealistic in character.[2] Because certain elements of the Romantic literary tradition, including its moral idealism, buttressed the cause of racial equality and justice, black novelists initially adopted and then clung to Romantic literary techniques.[3] Many Afro-American novels were written as counterstereotypes to the romanticized portrayals of slavery in plantation school fiction and to its libelous depiction of Negro character. The novels were deliberately constructed in the same Romantic, fictional terms. For example, black novelists found the conventions of melodrama compatible with race protest and their spiritual uplift work. Melodrama's typically broad characterization and emphasis on action was very compatible with fictional polemics. The same compatibility explains why early novels by black women display strict adherence to conventions of the Genteel Tradition. The portrayal of morally irreproachable, usually light-skinned heroes and heroines accomplished in a stroke a number of early black fiction's most immediate goals. The light-skinned mulatto character, while still a racial figure, was one with which the white reader could identify. The problems of racial caste, in the context of this character's experience, appeared to the reader, the novelists hoped, all the more horrible, irrational, and unjust. Not only did tales concerning the triumphs and woes of light-skinned mulattoes refute the black stereotype but they also promulgated, for the benefit of black Americans, a moral and social ideal.

Not until the period of the Harlem Renaissance, beginning in the early 1920s, did Afro-American artists rebel against their charge to show Afro-American life and character in only an idealistic and exemplary manner. Now, Afro-American writers and artists insisted upon affirming the worth of black culture on its own terms, and they endeavored to ground their art in the actual experience of the majority of black Americans rather than in the narrow and unrepresentative experience of a tiny, middle-class minority. Most black novelists began to search for unique qualities in the racial character that could be exploited in their art. The more authentic-seeming embodiments of race-life they discovered in black men and women of the lower class were soon to replace completely the mannered, middle-class figures typical of novels of the earlier period. The expressions of Puritan morality prevalent in the earlier works were summarily repudiated in favor of more robust, spontaneous characters and the down-to-earth mores of the folk. Jean Toomer, whose *Cane* first signaled this new trend in Afro-American fiction, announced a period of racial self-celebration: "Shake your curly wool-blossoms, nigger. Open your liver lips to the lean, white Spring. Stir the root-life of a withered people. Call them from their houses, and teach them to dream."[4]

Cane, like many other black novels of the 1920s, was redolently "primitive." Primitivism in black fiction was a rejection of the protest tradition's prim superficiality in a conscious attempt to focus on the black American as an unsullied and irrepressible child of nature.[5] Its exponents, writers of the Harlem School, saw among unlettered black folk a kind of racial truth which, transformed into art, would constitute the black American's unique contribution to American civilization. The defiant use of such material on the part of black writers despite its close resemblance to the racial stereotype and over the hot objections of black conservatives, was an expression of the period's intense cultural nationalism as well as an attempt by creative artists to break free of restrictions artificially imposed on their work. In the process of this struggle, writers and poets began to produce conscious works of art rather than propaganda. These avant-garde writers exuberantly laid claim to all the prerogatives of the creative artist; they asserted their right and intention to explore the black artist's own literary province: the essence of Afro-American identity and heritage. In 1926, Langston Hughes proclaimed the Afro-American artist's declaration of independence:

We younger Negro artists who create now intend to express our in- dividual dark-skinned selves without fear or shame. If white people are pleased we are glad. If they are not, it doesn't matter. We know we are beautiful. And ugly too. . . . If colored people are pleased we are glad. If they are not, their displeasure doesn't matter either.[6]

In general, the novels of Afro-American women constitute a distinct countertendency to the artistic phase of the Harlem Renaissance. Black women novelists, in the years following the close of the First World War, reacted as to a crisis. Their an- ger and disappointment with the state of postwar race rela- tions, which included a huge increase in the incidence of lynching, is explicit in the fiction. Mary Spencer's *The Resent- ment*, Lillian Wood's *"Let My People Go,"* and Jessie Fauset's *There Is Confusion* show black women novelists firm in the conviction that the Afro-American novel should advance the racial cause in the same manner as in the past—that is, openly and within the context of the narrative.[7] Among black women novelists, the nationalism of the Harlem Renaissance period led to increased scrutiny and criticism of intraracial experi- ence and an even greater didactic emphasis.[8] Although they are as politically motivated and morally idealistic as in the former period, these novels are characterized more by realis- tic than romantic literary techniques.

The influence of naturalism and social realism were promi- nent influences on the black American novel during the 1930s. The Afro-American artist, according to Ralph Ellison, came to recognize "the themes and problems of Drieser, Sinclair, and London as relevant to Negro experience. In the stress of the Great Depression, the Negro artist became conscious of class as well as race, and his identification with the poverty-stricken masses led away from Harlem frivolity and toward re-discov- ery of his rural, and Southern roots."[9] Richard Wright's *Na- tive Son* (1940), the inspiration for a spate of naturalistic nov- els by other black authors, had itself been influenced by novels by Dos Passos, Farrell, Steinbeck, and Dreiser.[10] Yet, in novels such as *Native Son*, William Attaway's *Blood on the Forge* (1940), Carl Offord's *White Face* (1943), Chester Himes' *If He Hollers, Let Him Go* (1945), and Ann Petry's *The Street* (1946), the writers' primary concern is with the condition of the racial group. The protest orientation of the black novel was to be dramatically altered, however, when confronted by the humanitarian philosophy of the World War II years and the integration movement.[11]

Delegates to the first conference of Afro-American writers, convened in 1959 by the American Society for African Culture, noted the impact of integrationist thinking on Afro-American fiction. America's changed racial climate, stated Arthur P. Davis, "inadvertently dealt the Negro writer a crushing blow." "One must remember," said Davis, "that the protest tradition was no mere fad with the Negro writer. It was part of his respect, part of his philosophy of life, part of his inner-being."[12]

The black novelist's commitment to exploring racial concerns in fiction was profoundly challenged by the integration idea. Some writers, however, continued to discuss issues pertinent to the race but avoided the use of black characters.[13] Out of the press of these apparently conflicting values—race consciousness and racial integration—black novels of the latter forties and fifties achieved a breadth of theme that encompassed, and went beyond, the racial framework.[14] In William Gardner Smith's *The Last of the Conquerors*, for example, a black soldier must go abroad to experience freedom. Yet, "When we finish the book," writes Blyden Jackson, "we are at least as much aware of the beauty of the democratic ideal as we are of the baseness of those who sabotage it."[15] In addition to thematic breadth, post–World War II novels by black Americans display a wide range of literary techniques and a skillful blending of racial concerns and universal themes.

Yet, although black novelists now produced works that "subscribed to the principles of modern tragedy," these novels, as Carl Milton Hughes notes, are not marked by the sense of defeat and of irrevocable loss so common in contemporary American fiction.[16] Because the notion of human helplessness and social alienation did not and could not advance the racial

cause, Afro-American novelists refused to acknowledge that
which the white writer mourned. Their stories did not lament
the loss of a consistent and overarching ethical framework or
the increasingly diminished capacity of the modern man or
woman to exert moral force in the postwar world.[17] Of the disillusioned modern writer, Frederick Hoffman wrote:

The basic question troubling the modern novelist is that of moral form:
how does one define action, behavior? It needs a contest; mere im-
provisation of moral codes is a romantic strategem which may be
necessary at times but cannot forever satisfactorily define or justify
what we do. The *picaro* simply goes on and on.[18]

Afro-American writers severely criticized the mainstream
novelist's easy abdication of social responsibility. The modern
American novel, Ralph Ellison charged, no longer created or
extended the national myth. The American novelist, in re-
stricting himself to his own personal myth is "defeated as a
manipulator of profound social passions."[19] The significance of
his own *Invisible Man*, Ellison says, is "its attempt to return
to the mood of personal responsibility for democracy which
typified the best of our nineteenth-century fiction."[20]

Julian Mayfield, author of *The Hit* (1957) and *The Long Night*
(1958), also decried the mainstream writer's abdication of social responsibility. He was contemptuous, therefore, of the idea
that the black writer should redirect his efforts in conformity
with those of mainstream writers. Rather, in his paper "Into
the Mainstream and Oblivion," Mayfield points to the modern
novel's unworthy preoccupation with the "foibles of suburban
living, the junior executive, dope addiction, homosexuality, incest, and divorce." In ignoring the responsibility of each individual to society, the mainstream writer, according to Mayfield, had cut himself off from a fully human engagement with
life. Furthermore, he contended, the deficits of mainstream
fiction were those of American society in general and were not
likely to change.[21]

These statements by Ellison, Mayfield, and Davis and black
novels themselves illustrate the relationship between Afro-
American fiction, the racial policies obtaining within the race,

and those prevailing in the larger society. Mayfield spoke presciently of integration and the younger generation of black writers when he said: "Young writers are wiser than most of our church, civic, and political leaders, who are pushing with singular concentration toward one objective: integration."[22] His skeptical view of integration anticipated that of black critics and writers of the sixties who, asserting that the myth of American democracy had run its course and that Western civilization itself was dying, turned once again for answers to a philosophy of black political and cultural nationalism: "If the dream he [the black man] chased for three centuries is now dying even for white Americans, he would be wise to consider alternative objectives."[23]

The drama of the Afro-American novel, then, appears to involve the search for forms and themes which, for the black American, are at once morally, politically, and artistically valid. In novels written during and for a period after the Second World War, humanitarian philosophy, with its affirmation of the worth of each individual, temporarily enabled this artistic/political dilemma to be resolved. By embracing and extending the novelists' racial concerns, it made possible a synthesis of strictly racial and universally human themes. Drawing on ideas about the integrity of the individual, Afro-American novelists found a solution to a number of black fiction's most common aesthetic problems. These problems sprang from the black novel's grounding in collective rather than universal values. According to Edward Bland, black American fiction had failed to draw on "orientations in our culture." For much of its history, it failed to "incorporate humanistic notions about the dignity of the individual and human brotherhood.[24] Thus, the black novel whose smallest unit was the group rather than the individual, was dominated by plot and typically weak in character development.

As abruptly as the literary approaches appropriate to the protest tradition became outmoded when confronted by the integration idea, the literature influenced by integrationist thinking was challenged by the cultural nationalism of the 1960s and its particular vision of race pride and racial separatism. And, if contemporary mainstream fiction found its origins in the modern artist's increasing social alienation, then the new literature of black nationalism pessimistically dismissed the larger culture entirely. As a mirror of Afro-American political thought, it proposed the artist's total engagement with the black community.[25]

The black American novel, then, has diverged from prevailing literary trends under the influence of a political context and as a result of the artist's conscious use or rejection of literary styles and approaches prevailing in the larger culture. It is this political dimension and orientation of Afro-American fiction which has accounted for some of its unique literary patterns. In these patterns lie part of the key to understanding its meaning.[26] Moreover, to a large degree, these patterns further define and explain the important differences between Afro-American and mainstream American fiction.

Notes

1. According to Alfred Kazin (*On Native Ground*, 1956), modern fiction originates in the 1880s and 1890s when industrialism and urbanization led to the emergence of a new metropolitan culture. The alienation of the modern American writer, Kazin thought, was rooted in the moral crisis posed by this new era. John Aldridge (*After the Lost Generation*, 1951) discusses the writer's alienation from public values. Nona Balakian and Charles Simmons (*The Creative Present*, 1963) and Ihab Hassan (*Contemporary American Literature*, 1973) speak of the writer's accommodation to the conditions of the modern age and new sense of poise.

2. "Not only did the early novelist write exclusively within the Romantic tradition but he chose melodrama—the very caricature of the tradition—as his principal literary vehicle." (Bone, 21)

3. There are aspects of naturalism in Paul Lawrence Dunbar's *The Sport of the Gods* and W.E.B. Du Bois' *Quest of the Golden Fleece*. And, while there are aspects of realism in *Autobiography of An Ex-Colored Man* by James Weldon Johnson, each of these narratives also contains melodramatic features.

4. Toomer, 104.

5. The following critical studies contain varying opinions regarding the effect of primitivism in the black novel: Bone, 57–61; Gloster, 160; Glicksberg, 47–53.

6. Williams and Harris, eds., *Amistad 1*, 305.

7. While male writers of the Harlem Renaissance, except for Walter White and W.E.B. Du Bois, turned away from propaganda fiction and celebrated Afro-American folk life, as expressed as well in the black metropolis, black female novelists clearly continued to adhere to the older, missionary goals of Negro writing. They were still concerned with what Alain Locke called the "inner objectives" of the "New Negro" period.

The Negro today is inevitably moving forward under the control largely of his own objectives. . . . Those of his outer life are happily already well formulated, for they are none other than the ideals of American institutions and democracy. . . . Up to the present, one may adequately see the Negro's inner objectives as an attempt to repair a damaged group psychology and reshape a warped social perspective. (Locke, 10)

8. See Chapter II.
9. Bone, 118.
10. The social criticism in *Native Son*, according to Houston Baker, mirrors that of other problem novels of the thirties.

Like the muckrakers and other protest novelists of his age, Wright depicted a deplorable social environment. . . . Bigger Thomas, like Sinclair's Jurgis Rudkus, Dreiser's Clyde Griffiths, and Farrell's Studs Lonigan, is an American victim. (Baker, 207)

11. Actually, according to Ralph Bunche, the movement for integration began immediately at the close of the First World War. It was spearheaded in the South by the Commission on Interracial Cooperation located in Atlanta, Georgia. The Negro Committee was called together by Major Moton of Tuskegee. The commission's primary program was the training of black and white leaders for educational work in race relations. These men, nearly half of whom were clergy of varying denominations, were to hold national, state, county, and local conferences to encourage interracial cooperation. Initially, they worked through the churches to aid in the readjustment of returing soldiers. Once past these early stages, the commission determined to work permanently for interracial goodwill. The movement was not confined either to the South or to the efforts of the commission. By 1940, when Ralph Bunche prepared the memoranda for the Myrdal study concerning tactics and strategies of interracial organizations, he assessed the work of numbers of organizations throughout the nation. Bunche, III, 450; IV, 538–639.
12. American Society of African Culture, 38, 63.

13. Examples of raceless novels are: Ann Petry's *Country Place* (1947); William Gardner Smith's *Anger At Innocence* (1950); Zora Neale Hurston's *Seraph on the Suwanee* (1948); Chester Hime's *Cast the First Stone* (1952).

14. Prominent among these are Ellison's *Invisible Man* (1952) and Baldwin's *Go Tell It on the Mountain* (1953).

15. Jackson, 186.

16. Hughes, 32.

17. Robert H. Walker notes the concern of postwar novelists with evaluating individual behavior in light of the collectivity of the age. All the worthy novels of the Second World War, he states, are concerned with "the question of individual responsibility in a world where the questions are posed with seeming impersonality and the answers can be met only by collective action." (LXV, 9)

According to Saul Bellow, the bitterness of the contemporary novelist at the loss of a moral frame reveals an unearned self-indulgence. Bellow claims that "what the young American writer most often appears to feel is *his* own misfortune. The injustice is done to *his* talent if life is brutish and ignorant. . . . Neither for himself nor for his fellows does he attack power and injustice directly and hotly." (XV, 14)

18. Hoffman, 227.

19. Ellison, *Shadow and Act*, 52–56.

20. Ibid., 111.

21. American Society for African Culture, 32.

22. Ibid., 30.

23. Ibid., 31.

24. Bland, XLIII, 328.

25. Larry Neal, in an article that appeared in *The Drama Review* cogently states the philosophy of the Black Aesthetic:

The Black Arts Movement is radically opposed to any concept of the artist that alienates him from his community. Black Art is the aesthetic and spiritual sister of the Black Power concept. As such, it envisions art that speaks directly to the needs and aspirations of Black America. In order to perform this task, the Black Arts Movement proposes a radical reordering of the western cultural aesthetic. It proposes a separate symbolism, mythology, critique, and iconology. The Black Arts and the Black Power concept both relate broadly to the Afro-American's desire for self-determination and nationhood. Both concepts are nationalistic. One is concerned with the relationship between art and politics; the other with the art of politics. . . . Recently, these two movements have begun to merge. (Neal, XII, 30)

26. Post–World War II critics examined literary patterns in black fiction more closely than previously. Blyden Jackson finds irony to be the black novel's presiding genius. In his study of short fiction by Afro-Americans, Bone points to what he terms pastoral and antipastoral patterns in Afro-American short fiction.

Roger Rosenblatt (*Black Fiction*, 1974) identifies a cyclical thematic pattern throughout the whole of black fiction and urges literary critics to take into account the black novel's distinguishing literary patterns and motifs, not only its sociohistorical reflection of Afro-American life.

The point to emphasize . . . is not only that there has been a correspondence between the experiences and the stories, but that the stories have been similar to each other as well, that indeed, while a number of literary movements and digressions was occurring in the nation at large over the past eighty years, black fiction has continued to function with patterns peculiarly its own. It is the existence of the patterns, not simply of common external experience which makes the subject real. (Rosenblatt, 2)

V

SUMMARY

For much of their history, novels by black American women have been more concerned with racial issues than with art. Because of the concern of black women novelists with social rather than with artistic goals, the vivid social and political content of their stories everywhere confronts the reader. While the protest function of the black novel has been long recognized, crucial to an understanding of black women's novels is recognition of the novelists' engagement with intraracial issues, which is a second major thrust in their fiction. Black women novelists have been deeply committed to the racial cause, and their fidelity to the service ideal informs a majority of the novels they have authored. Novels by black women which appeared during the 1920s were more influenced by the nationalistic sentiment of the Harlem Renaissance than by its artistic thrust. The prescriptive character of the stories, even of those novels published after the Second World War, is surprisingly forthright and insistent.

From the outset, however, black women novelists embraced issues far deeper than those which concerned the Afro-American's social, economic, or political status. The novelists early recognized and tried to repair, through their fiction, the damage that slavery and oppression had dealt to the black American's sense of self-esteem. Their recognition of the race's inner needs had a potent effect on the content of the novels which, while it was directed outward to the larger society as protest and propaganda, was aimed inward to the black community and was meant to be redemptive.

This deeper motive, and the novelists' sense of racial peril, lends an added tone of urgency to many of the novels. Viewing the race question as a matter of black survival, black women novelists couched their fictional remedies in ethical and moral terms. Their prescriptions regarding racial self-help, the practice of "passing," and intraracial color prejudice sprung from a race-conscious ethical system and forcefully illustrate early black fiction's preindividualistic, or communal, values. Not until after the Second World War did black women novelists in significant numbers achieve in their narratives a synthesis of aesthetic and political concerns. The postwar period witnessed the appearance of many novels by black women that are both race-conscious and universally meaningful works of art.

Among all the novels studied, the work of Zora Neale Hurston stands out as unique. *Jonah's Gourd Vine* and *Moses, Man of the Mountain* capture the black woman novelist's preoccupation with intraracial issues and her faith in self-help. Hurston's second novel, *Their Eyes Were Watching God*, signalled the black female novelist's concern with universal, as well as group-minded, values. It is the first novel authored by a black American woman which adequately conveys the rich complexity of race in the life of the black individual.

Still, there were many writers throughout the history of novel writing by black American women who simply wanted to serve as witnesses to their peculiar American experience and who struggled to communicate this experience in print. It is clear that writing a novel gave many of them a deeply satisfying sense of self. Lucy Mae Turner, for example, typed *The Flaming Sword* (1935) single-spaced on half-size paper, sketching by hand in ink a sword on the handmade cover. Hoping her story would reach an audience which she could not then envision, Turner wrote in her preface:

Since I have been colored myself for lo! these many years, in fact since I first saw the light of day, I am moved to write this novel of Negro life. Since I am poor and without prestige, I am moved to publish it myself.

The brook will find a channel to the sea and the human mind will find an outlet to the public. It is only the stones of all creation that are dumb, and sometimes they seem to move. So often the thought and sentiments of Negroes are voiced for us by kindly white people that very seldom does our voice find public utterance. But I am one of God's black children who believes in doing her own talking.

. . .

So children, here it is, with
  affectionate friendliness
    to ALL Humanity

(Turner, n.p.)

CHRONOLOGICAL LIST OF NOVELS AND STORIES

1859:   Wilson, Harriet H. *Our Nig; or, Sketches from the Life of a Free Black in a Two-Story White House, North, Showing that Slavery's Shadows Fall Even There*. Boston: George C. Rand & Avery, 1859; 2nd edition, New York: Vintage Books, 1983.

1891:   Kelly, Emma Dunham. *Megda*. Boston: James H. Earle, 1891.

1892:   Harper, Frances E. W. *Iola Leroy, or Shadows Uplifted*. Philadelphia: Garrigues Brothers, 1892.

1894:   Johnson, Amelia E. *The Hazeley Family*. Philadelphia: American Baptist Publication Society, 1894.

1900:   Hopkins, Pauline Elizabeth. *Contending Forces: A Romance Illustrative of Negro Life, North and South*. Boston: Colored Co-Operative Publishing Co., 1900.

1902:   ———. *Of One Blood: or The Hidden Self*. Twelve installments in *The Colored American Magazine*, beginning November 1902.

1918:   Fleming, Sara Lee Brown. *Hope's Highway*. New York: Neale Publishing Co., 1918.

1920:   Wright, Zara. *Black and White Tangled Threads*. Chicago: The Author, 1920.

1920:   ———. *Kenneth*. Chicago: The Author, 1920.

1921:   Spencer, Mary Etta. *The Resentment*. Philadelphia: A.M.E. Book Concern, 1921.

1921:   Wood, Lillian E. *"Let My People Go."* Philadelphia: A.M.E. Book Concern, 1921.

1924:   Fauset, Jessie Redmond. *There Is Confusion.* New York: Boni & Liverwright, 1924.

1927:   ———. *Plum Bun.* New York: Frederick A. Stokes Co., 1927.

1928:   Larsen, Nella. *Quicksand.* New York: A. Knopf, 1928.

1929:   ———. *Passing.* New York: A. Knopf, 1929.

1931:   Fauset, Jessie Redmond. *The Chinaberry Tree.* New York: Frederick A. Stokes Co., 1931.

1932:   ———. *Comedy, American Style.* New York: Frederick A. Stokes Co., 1932.

1934:   Hurston, Zora Neale. *Jonah's Gourd Vine.* Philadelphia: Lippincott, 1934.

1935:   Turner, Lucy Mae. *The Flaming Sword.* East St. Louis, Ill.: 1935. (typewritten)

1937:   Hurston, Zora Neale. *Their Eyes Were Watching God.* Philadelphia: Lippincott, 1937.

1938:   Gilbert, Mercedes. *Aunt Sara's Wooden God.* Boston: The Christopher Publishing House, 1938.

1939:   Hurston, Zora Neale. *Moses, Man of the Mountain.* Philadelphia: Lippincott, 1939.

Pitts, Gertrude. *Tragedies of Life.* Newark, N.J.: The Author, 1939.

1941:   Graham, Katheryn Campbell. *Under the Cottonwood.* New York: Wendell Malliet & Co., 1941.

1942:   Nelson, Annie Greene. *After the Storm.* Columbia, S.C.: Hampton Publishing Co., 1942.

1944:   ———. *The Dawn Appears.* Columbia, S.C.: Hampton Publishing Co., 1944.

1945:   Wood, Odella Phelps. *High Ground.* New York: The Exposition Press, 1945.

1946:   Petry, Ann. *The Street.* Boston: Houghton Mifflin Co., 1946.

1947:   ———. *Country Place.* Boston: Houghton Mifflin Co., 1947.

1948:   Hurston, Zora Neale. *Seraph on the Suwanee.* New York: Scribner's Sons, 1948.

West, Dorothy. *The Living Is Easy.* Boston: Houghton Mifflin Co., 1948.

1951:   Finch, Amanda. *Back Trail: A Novella of Love in the South.* New York: The Williams-Frederick Press, 1951.

Rosebrough, Sadie Mae. *Wasted Travail.* New York: Vantage Press, 1951.

1952:   Dickens, Dorothy Lee. *Black On the Rainbow*. New York: Pageant, 1952.
1953:   Arnold, Ethel Nishua. *She Knew No Evil*. New York: Vantage Press, 1953.

Brooks, Gwendolyn. *Maud Martha*. New York: Popular Library, 1953.

Petry, Ann. *The Narrows*. Boston: Houghton Mifflin Co., 1953.

Wamble, Thelma. *All in the Family*. New York: New Voices Publishing Co., 1953.

1954:   Jordan, Elsie. *Strange Sinner*. New York: Pageant, 1954.

Wallace, Elizabeth West. *Scandal at Daybreak*. New York: Pageant, 1954.

1955:   Humphrey, Lillie Muse. *Aggie*. New York: Vantage Press, 1955.

1956:   Beechwood, Mary. *Memphis Jackson's Son*. Boston: Houghton Mifflin Co., 1956.

Childress, Alice. *Like One of the Family*. Brooklyn: Independence, 1956.

Daniels, Lucy. *Caleb, My Son*. New York: Lippincott, 1956.

1957:   Shaw, Letty M. *Angel Mink*. New York: Comet, 1957.

1959:   Bellinger, Claudia. *Wolf Kitty*. New York: Vantage Press, 1959.

1959:   Marshall, Paule. *BrownGirl, Brownstones*. New York: Random House, 1959.

Vaught, Estella V. *Vengeance Is Mine*. New York: Comet, 1959.

1960:   Cotton, Ella Earls. *Queen of Persia, the Story of Esther Who Saved Her People*. New York: Exposition, 1960.

Shores, Minnie T. *Publicans and Sinners*. New York: Comet, 1960.

1962:   Brown, Mattye Jeanette. *The Reign of Terror*. New York: Vantage, 1962.

Clinton, Dorothy Randle. *The Maddening Scar*. Boston: Christopher Press, 1962.

Skinner, Theodosia B. *Ice Cream From Heaven*. New York: Vantage, 1962.

1963:   Roberson, Sadie L. *Killer of the Dream*. New York: Comet, 1963.

Vroman, Mary E. *Esther*. New York: Bantam, 1963.

1964:   Forte, Christine [Christine Forster]. *A View From the Hill*. New York: Vantage, 1964.

1964: (*Continued*)

    Hunter, Kristin. *God Bless the Child*. New York: Scribner's, 1964.

    La Hon, Vyola Therese. *The Big Lie*. New York: Vantage, 1964.

    Washington, Doris V. *Yulan*. New York: Carlton, 1964.

CONCERNS AND THEMES

Table 1
Summary Chart

Themes	Chapter		
	I	II	III
Protest Aimed at American Society	87.5	77.7	78.1
Strategies for Advancement	75.0	66.6	37.5
Concern with Special Groups	75.0	66.6	31.2
Intra-Racial Concerns	12.5	66.6	40.6
Religious Behavior and Values	100.0	50.0	28.1

Note: This chart (Table 1) summarizes the major concerns and themes of the novels and the percentage of their appearance during each of the periods; 1891–1920; 1921–1945; 1946–1965. Table 2 provides a further breakdown of the overall themes into topics along with the percentage of their appearance in novels of each period.

Table 2

Topics and Percentages of Appearance

Topic	Percentage
Chapter I	
Protest Aimed at American Society	87.5%
Racial Discrimination Discrimination in the North in housing, education, employment; in the South in education and in the legal system.	27.5
Anti-Negro Propaganda (novels, newspapers, magazines, sermons, lectures, etc.)	22.2
Lynching and Other Forms of Anti-Negro Violence	22.2
Disfranchisement	16.7
Color Prejudice	11.1
Total	100.0%
Strategies for Advancement	75.0%
Moral Elevation of Afro-Americans	25.0
Racial Solidarity (race loyalty in fair-skinned mulattoes, altruistic dedication of successful Black Americans)	15.0
Education	15.0
White Benevolence	15.0
African Emigration (unfavorable reactions)	10.0
Race Pride	5.0
Militant Protest	5.0
Education of Whites on Matters of Race	5.0
Temperance	5.0
Total	100.0 %
Concern with Special Groups	75.0%
Afro-American Women (sexual victimization)	33.3
Women in General	33.3

Table 2
(Continued)

Topic	Percentage
Mulattoes	22.2
Black Male Professionals (lack of civil protection and respect)	11.2
Total	100.0 %
Intra-Racial Concerns	12.5%
Disunity among Northern and Southern Black Americans	33.3
Bias Against Mulattoes	33.3
Color Bias (against dark-skinned Afro-Americans)	33.3
Total	100.0%
Religious Behavior and Values	100.0%
Christianity (proselytizing of whites in the interest of racial justice; moral elevation of Negroes)	50.0
Christianity (treatment of general precepts unrelated to social issues)	25.0
Expressions of Faith in Divine Intervention (as solution to problems of race)	12.5
Expression of Faith in Spiritual Power of a Collective Racial Spirit	12.5
Total	100.0%
Chapter II **Protest Aimed at American Society**	77.7%
Racial Discrimination (Northern discrimination in housing, education, employment; discrimination in Southern courts)	37.5
Race Prejudice	25.0
Peonage	18.7
Racism	6.3
Lynching	6.3

Table 2
(Continued)

Topic	Percentage
Inequality of Women	6.2
Total	100.0%
Strategies for Advancement	66.6%
Middle-Class Achievement (education, material security, respectability, social class)	28.5
Racial Solidarity (racial uplift through self-help, race loyalty in fair-skinned mulattoes)	21.4
Black Leadership	11.9
Race Pride	11.9
White Benevolence	7.1
Associationism (NAACP)	4.8
Exercise of the Franchise	4.8
Emigration to the North	4.0
Racial Integration	2.4
Communism (unfavorable comment)	2.4
Total	100.0%
Intra-Racial Concerns	66.6%
Intra-Racial Color Bias	57.1
Passing	28.6
Education of Afro-American Youth (unfavorable commentary on the Tuskegee model)	7.2
Morality of Black American Youth	7.1
Total	100.0%
Concern with Special Groups	66.6%
Black American Women (sexual victimization, helplessness and dependency, emotional suffering)	58.3%
Black GIs (discrimination in armed services, mistreatment of returned soldiers at home)	33.3

Table 2
(Continued)

Topics	Percentage
Women in General (sexual inequality)	8.4
<u>Religious Behavior and Values</u>	50.0%
Relationship between Christian Faith, Moral Behavior and Afro-American Freedom	53.4
Role of the Church in Afro-American Life	46.6
Total	100.0%
Chapter III <u>Protest Aimed at American Society</u>	78.1%
Race Prejudice	46.7
The Urban Ghetto	17.8
Lynching and Other Anti-Negro Violence	11.1
Anti-Semitism	8.9
Racial Segregation	6.7
Employment Discrimination	4.4
Parochialism and Narrow-mindedness	4.4
Total	100.0%
<u>Strategies for Advancement</u>	37.5%
Education	17.4
Religious Faith and Morality	17.4
Emigration to the North	13.0
Militant Protest	8.6
Inter-racial Brotherhood	8.6
Racial Solidarity	8.6
Race Pride	4.4
Legal Challenge in the Courts	4.4
Loyalty and Patriotism	4.4
Communism	4.4

Table 2
(Continued)

Topic	Percentage
Socialism	4.4
Racial Integration	4.4
Total	100.0%
Concern with Special Groups	31.2%
Afro-American Women (sexual victimization, lack of male protectors, lack of respect, poverty, dependency)	57.2
Black Immigrants in the Urban North	14.3
Mulattoes	14.3
American GI's (Black and white)	7.1
Women in General (sexual inequality)	7.1
Total	100.0%
Intra-Racial Concerns	40.6%
Psychological Effects of Racism	30.0
Color Bias Among Blacks	20.0
Extreme Consciousness of Social Class	10.0
Passing	5.0
Education of Black Southern Youth	5.0
Morality of Afro-American Youth	5.0
Total	100.0%
Religious Behavior and Values	28.1%
Christianity (as solution to problems of interracial conflict)	62.5
Moral Dilemmas Unique to the Racially Oppressed	25.0
Psychological Origins of Religious Fanaticism	12.5
Total	100.0%

BIBLIOGRAPHICAL NOTE

This study required the compilation of a complete bibliography of novels written before 1965 by black American women. The list of works included relies primarily on bibliographies contained in: *A Century of Fiction by American Negroes, 1854–1952* by Maxwell Whiteman; *The Negro Novel in America* by Robert Bone; *American Negro Fiction* by Frank Deodene and William P. French; *Black American Literature* by Robert Whitlow; "Afro-American Fiction: A Checklist; 1853–1970," by Robert A. Corrigan. The latter appeared in, among other places, the *Mid-Continent American Studies Journal* (Fall 1970).

Excluded from the list are novels by Felice Swados (*House of Fury*) and Virginia Harris (*Wedding Trimmin's*). Although Whiteman, as Bone points out, lists Swados and Harris in his bibliography of black writers, these novelists are identified as white authors in the Howard University Spingarn Collection. This study also excludes *What's Wrong With Lottery?* by Ruth Thompson Barnard. This book, which is frequently included in bibliographies of black fiction, is actually a nonfiction tract about the evil of gambling.

Bibliographies citing *Megda*, a novel by Emma Dunham Kelley, erroneously give its publication date as 1892. The novel was actually published in 1891, one year prior to Frances E. W. Harper's *Iola Leroy*, the novel long thought to be the first published in the United States by a black American woman. Recent research by Henry Gates, Jr., which establishes the authorship by a black woman of *Our Nig* (1859) pushes this date back even further.

I was unable to examine Maggie Shaw Fullilove's *Who Was Responsible?* (1919), Fay Liddle Coolidge's *Black Is White* (1958), Helen Hunter's *Magnificent White Men* (1964), and Amelia Johnson's *Martina Meriden* (1901). Another novel by Johnson often referred to as *In God's Way* (1891) could be the same work as her *Clarence and Corinne; or God's Way* published in 1890 by the American Baptist Publication Society. Neither *Clarence and Corinne* nor *The Hazeley Family*, which is also by Johnson, contains any internal evidence to indicate their authorship by a black American.

This study, whose dates exclude in-depth consideration of the antebellum autobiographical novel, *Our Nig*, is based on fifty-eight of the sixty-four novels known to have been written before 1965 by black American women.

The bibliography of secondary sources is a partial listing of works consulted. It contains critical analyses of black American literature, studies that were especially helpful in defining the social, historical, and cultural context in which the novels were written, and those which focus directly on Afro-American social and political thought.

ANNOTATED BIBLIOGRAPHY

For the convenience of the reader, the annotated bibliography is arranged alphabetically by title. See Appendix A for complete citations, listed chronologically.

After the Storm. (Nelson, Annie Greene), 1942.

An extremely gauche, inspirational tale about a simple Christian girl who, after becoming pregnant out of wedlock, later recovers her social position through marriage to a physician. When forced to leave home by her mother following the discovery of her pregnancy, Nanette is befriended by a stranger, Maw Jennie, who is impressed by her Christian piety. Numerous demonstrations of Nanette's faith and charity occur as she awaits the birth of her child. As the fates would have it, the child is born dead; the attending doctor falls in love with Nanette and asks her for her hand in marriage. From her exalted position as wife of a physician, Nanette is free to lead a life of community service, and her detractors are silenced. The tale appears to be loosely based on fact. In his introduction to the story, Professor Baumgardener stoutly defends a man named Reverend Holbrook, Nanette's seducer, writing that Holbrook is simply an average man who becomes involved with Nanette only after the death of his wife.

Aggie. (Humphrey, Lillie Muse), 1955.

Aggie, a dedicated young school teacher, goes to her first job in a rural town in southeastern Florida. She and other young teachers face a community extremely hostile both to teachers and to education. Female teachers are harassed by older, married women who are jealous of the young teachers' social status and fear their youthful sexual attractiveness. Aggie and her friends endure physical assault by parents and the threatened loss of their jobs. Aggie persists, however, trying to improve the education of the children by reaching out to their parents. Hers is a timid but kindly life, and her views about education stress the responsibility of the teacher to overcome the backwardness of the community. In the story, she criticizes some teachers for neglecting their duties. This autobiographical tale reflects the author's pride in her own accomplishments as a rural schoolteacher and her desire to teach others how to overcome the difficulties of a similar situation.

All in the Family. (Wamble, Thelma), 1953.

Depression era hardships have a liberalizing effect on the attitudes of a well-to-do, white family in which the central character, an unmarried physician named Mark, fails to recognize his own homosexual leanings but maintains a sympathetic, scientifically objective attitude toward Shelby, a "pseudohermaphrodite." As the family learns, through Mark's influence, to accept Shelby, they also learn to accept his friend, an Afro-American law student. The author treats the subject of homosexuality with great indirection and appears to advocate more liberal views in this area of sexuality in the hope of fostering more tolerant racial attitudes as well.

Angel Mink. (Shaw, Letty), 1957.

A raceless novel about the evils of slum life in which each character's dominant personality trait is revealed in a telltale name. The story takes place in Sen District, also referred to as Squalorville. A young girl named Angel Mink is mistreated by an aunt whom she believes to be her mother. When Angel's hard-working father dies, Dollar (the aunt) steals the insurance money and, later, tries to force Angel to become a prostitute. When Angel runs away, Dollar has her thrown into a juvenile detention facility. The local court, however, proves to be Angel's salvation. Upon discovering that her grandmother and Dollar have tried to defraud her of yet another insurance claim, she informs the authorities, and the court places her in a loving foster home.

Aunt Sara's Wooden God. (Gilbert, Mercedes), 1938.

A story of color and Afro-American life in Byron, Georgia, written in dialect and told from the point of view of the folk. A mother's adoration of her light-skinned son blinds her to his faults and prevents her from appreciating the decent character of his darker brother. While Sara believes William is in Macon preparing himself for a life in the ministry, he is actually gambling and fraternizing with the town's lowest marginal types. His involvement in a robbery at the place where his brother works leads to the brother's conviction. While the innocent brother works on a chain gang, William tries to seduce his brother's fiancée. Eventually William repents and, after a period of manly work in a sawmill, comes home to die of tuberculosis. He dies in the arms of his grief stricken mother who, incredibly, never realizes he has ever violated her trust.

Back Trail: A Novella of Love in the South. (Finch, Amanda), 1951.

The curious tale of a man who courts a plain girl in order to be close to her younger, prettier sister. On the morning of George and Sarah's wedding day, George elopes with Baby, the younger girl. Baby dies during the first year of their marriage, leaving a child whom George rears alone. Believing that her sister bewitched George with her yellow skin, Sarah leads a life of bitterness and hate. In 1949, forty-nine years later, George and Sarah meet again, and this time George goes through with the marriage. Finch apparently intended to show something of the irony of life, perhaps by recounting a story that has the ring of truth.

The Big Lie. (La Hon, Vyola Therese), 1964.

Following the passage of the 1954 Civil Rights Act, a young lawyer decides to return with his family to the South of his youth. Juda Johnson's decision is in accord with a family tradition of fighting against the "Big Lie," the racist idea of inherent black inferiority. Juda's legal training, he believes, can now be used to aid Southern black folk in the fight for adequate schooling.

Black and White Tangled Threads. (Wright, Zara), 1920.

A melodramatic tale in which Zoleeta Andrews, a beautiful heiress, discovers her mixed blood on the eve of her engagement to Lord Blankleigh, a handsome English nobleman. Zoleeta's aunt wants her own daughter, Catherine, to marry Blankleigh; and through her machinations, Zoleeta is kidnapped and held in a tower. Catherine, however, marries Guy Randolph, later abandoning him along with their baby daughter when she learns of his mixed blood. Meanwhile, Zoleeta is rescued and marries Blankleigh. They have a happy life together in England, but after eighteen years, Zoleeta feels compelled to return to the American South to lecture white audiences about the race question. She cannot live at ease as a white in England while black Americans are mistreated in her native land.

Black on the Rainbow. (Dickens, Dorothy Lee), 1952.

A story of "passing" in which the heroine fails to find the stardom she seeks as a dancer on the New York stage. When Hilda Parker's racial identity is revealed, she is thrown out of the home of the Jewish couple who were overseeing what appeared to be a promising career, not only on the stage but also in New York society. Afflicted with poor judgment, Hilda joins a dance review troupe bound for Europe and is seduced by the manager who promises her marriage. During an argument in a nightclub, the manager slashes Hilda's face with a knife, whereupon she returns to Columbus, Georgia, penniless and a failure. There Hilda, who expects to be shunned by the community, at last finds her niche when an old friend, now a minister, asks her to marry him. Hilda becomes a pious supporter of her husband and of his ultra-conservative views about means to the resolution of racial issues.

BrownGirl, Brownstones. (Marshall, Paule), 1959; 1970.

In 1920, Deighton and Silla Boyce come as newlyweds from Barbados to a cold-water flat in Brooklyn. Following in the wake of the Dutch-English and the Scotch-Irish, they are among the new wave of immigrants to the area. Silla, like her West Indian friends, is determined to achieve economic security in America, a desire symbolized by owning a brownstone. Young Selina, preferring the easygoing, romantic attitude of her father, finds herself in endless conflict with her mother. Until Selina understands her mother's iron determination not to have their dreams defeated by prejudice, she hates the single-minded, acquisitive passion she sees in Silla and other West Indian women. Selina soon discovers that she is very much like Silla. However, she refuses to be spiritually constrained by goals that are solely materialistic. She resolves to use the strength she has learned from her mother and the other West Indians, especially the women, to find a broader, more personally expansive life outside the ghetto.

Caleb, My Son. (Daniels, Lucy), 1956.

A father in the South kills his own son because the son's provocative behavior threatens not only the welfare of his family but that of everyone in the black community. Asa cannot understand his son Caleb's refusal to comply with his wishes or to use Asa as a model for his own life. Caleb, however, is contemptuous of Asa's choices and he refuses to be satisfied with a safe, but second-class station in life. Caleb meets secretly with a group of jobless young friends and together they contrive naive plots for attacking segregation. One such plan involves Caleb's openly dating a white girl. He refuses to obey when Asa orders him to stop. As Caleb and the girl walk down the street one evening, Asa shoots him in the back with a rifle. Caleb's mother and Asa's contemporaries silently assent. They know that Asa has followed an unwritten code whose purpose is to ensure the survival of the black community.

The Chinaberry Tree. (Fauset, Jessie Redmond), 1931.

To be accepted by the Negro elite of Redbrook, New Jersey, is Laurentine Strange's sole desire. Her mother's past liaison with a wealthy white man is a nearly insurmountable barrier despite the fact that mother and lover are long since dead. Yet another obstacle to Laurentine's hopes is her counsin Melissa, who lives in her home and whose own mother and father never married. Because of their family backgrounds, both Laurentine and Melissa lose their first, very desirable suitors. Laurentine's beauty, taste, and accomplishments are not sufficient to storm the middle-class barricades. Upon her marriage to Stephen Denleigh, however, Laurentine is "in" at last. Negro society in Redbrook proves as difficult to conquer as any in America.

Comedy, American Style. (Fauset, Jessie Redmond), 1932.

Olivia Cary's obsession with color destroys her marriage, her life, and the lives of two of her children. Having chosen her husband in order to have light-skinned children, Olivia is determined that her family will live unhampered by racial restrictions. She is defeated in her plans by the birth of a third child who has dark skin. After years of rejection by his mother, Oliver despairs and commits suicide. The weak-willed Teresa lives out an unhappy marriage to a Frenchman arranged by Olivia. Olivia, driven to flee everything of color, leaves her husband, only to live a lonely and poverty-stricken life in Europe. In all, the unrelenting examination of color in this novel lays bare a nearly obsessive concern with color on the part of the author.

Contending Forces. (Hopkins, Pauline Elizabeth), 1900.

An immigrant Bermuda planter brings about his own death and disaster to his family as a result of his plan gradually to manumit his seven hundred slaves. In this romance of the Montfort family, the author attempts to encompass over one hundred years of Afro-American history, beginning in the latter years of the eighteenth century. After the murder of their father, the Montfort children are separated from their mother (who kills herself by drowning) and from each other. One son disappears into England and another into the black race in America. Some years later, the American descendants, members of the Smith family, lead lives of calm struggle in Boston. Dora Smith makes friends with Sappho Clark, a mysterious personage in her mother's boarding house, who works quietly as a home typist. Sappho is trying to forget that before the war she was Madame Beaubean, a New Orleans creole who was kidnapped at fourteen and placed in a house of prostitution by an uncle. All ends well, however, as all the members of the family reunite, and the young people marry appropriate partners.

Country Place. (Petry, Ann), 1947.

Prejudice and mean spiritedness are the chief afflictions of a small Connecticut town. These attitudes affect everyone, especially black people, the Irish and Jews. Within a twenty-four-hour time span, certain townsfolk come to recognize the true nature of the town and take steps to correct its historical wrongs. Johnny Roane, a disillusioned GI, escapes a wife who was unfaithful during the war. Mearns Gramby, the mother-dominated son of the town's wealthiest family, is released from his bondage to the ancestral home and freed to practice his profession in New York. Mrs. Gramby gives her mansion to the family's faithful black servants and bequeaths a plot of land on Main Street to the Catholic church so that Irish Catholics might worship at a decent site. The attorney she chooses to draw up her will is a struggling young Jew.

The Dawn Appears. (Nelson, Annie Greene), 1944.

As explicitly devout as her first novel, this story by Annie Nelson is full of patriotic and religious sentiment. Nelson comments directly on the action of the story in brief, intrusive essays about morality, education, democracy, and race relations. Her own voice is the most imposing in the novel, much of which concerns community rituals—

quilting bees, revivals, preparation for spring planting—engaged in by black folk in the environs of Pee Dee, South Carolina. The first section of the novel assesses the moral stature of an unwed mother. The second charts the career of a married couple. Jack, the "thinker" in the story, overcomes his initial skepticism about black participation in World War II but vows to fight for democracy on two fronts, at home and abroad. When the war is over, he plans to become a minister and preach the gospel of brotherhood. Despite overblown patriotic rhetoric in the novel, it is religious faith rather than faith in American democracy that sustains Rachel and Jack and the Brown plantation black folk during the Second World War.

Esther. (Vroman, Mary E.), 1963.

The life of an expansive, lively young girl is nearly ruined when she is raped and impregnated by the son of her white employer. Faithful to a vow extracted by her grandmother before her death, Esther continues her education and becomes a nurse. She becomes socially prominent in Leemouth, Alabama, where she succeeds at improving medical care for black patients at the segregated hospital. She is initially less successful in resolving the conflict between herself and her husband regarding racial attitudes to be taught to their children. The dark side of Esther's personality goes unrecognized until she tries to strangle a white boy after discovering him in an innocent encounter with her daughter.

The Flaming Sword. (Turner, Lucy Mae), 1935.

A story about the folly of "passing" and the divisive power of color written by a granddaughter of Nat Turner. In fleeing the South, Henry Johnson abandons not only his racial identity but also his wife and child. For a time, he flourishes as an executive in the Barr Company of St. Louis but inevitably falls upon hard times. His patron dies; the Crash wipes out his savings; and the white girl he is dating turns out to be the property of gangsters. Too late, Henry decides to return home. Marie McRae, believing he is about to jilt her, has already laid plans to have him killed.

God Bless the Child. (Hunter, Kristin), 1964.

A young girl, determined to leave the poverty of the ghetto and live in a fine house, literally works herself to death in her successful effort to accomplish her goals. Rosie lives long enough to see the ghetto's encroachment on the formerly select neighborhood she has chosen. From a lawless, irrepressible child, Rosie has grown into a driven young woman who supports herself, her mother, and her grandmother by working long hours at whatever job—legal or illegal—she can find. She spends hundreds of dollars for luxuries trying to buy the love of her snobbish, self-centered grandmother, a servant who loves her white folks more than her own daughter or grandchild. Before years of exhaustion finally claim Rosie's life, her grip on reality is loosened. Her success at buying the magnificent old house leads to fantasies of becoming a millionaire. Rosie triumphs, however, in her victory over the emotional tyranny of her grandmother.

The Hazeley Family. (Johnson, Amelia E.), 1894.

A raceless novel in turgid prose written to illustrate the rewards of Christian virtue. Flora Hazeley goes to live with two of her aunts and, when the wealthier, kindly aunt dies, returns home to reform everyone in her family, including her mother. Improbable coincidences lead to reunions of old friends, the discovery of long-lost relatives, sudden conversions, etc. The story gives no indication of its authorship by a black American; the illustrations it contains depict white people.

High Ground. (Wood, Odella Phelps), 1944.

The story of a World War I veteran who reaffirms his earlier decision to fight for his country even though younger men question the country's right to their loyalty during World War II. Yet, Jim (James Crispus Attucks) Clayton is not unaware of racial injustice. The story's most effective passage describes the extremely careful and backbreaking labor involved in the harvest of tobacco. Jim and his wife Marthana leave the South when they learn that a year's work in the fields has netted their landlord a profit but has left them deeper in debt. Their lives are a fable of success, however, as they choose the high ground of personal struggle and optimism rather than the low road of bitterness and despair.

Hope's Highway. (Fleming, Sarah Lee Brown), 1918.

A fantastic, wishful story in which Tom Brinley rises to a position of Negro leadership upon his acceptance of the principalship of Vance (Tuskegee) Institute after the death of the founder, Enoch Vance (Booker T. Washington). Most of the story is centered in the consciousness of a young white woman who is sympathetic to the Southern black cause. Representing liberal white sentiment in the North, Grace Ennery saves Tom from unjust imprisonment and sees that he is educated at Oxford. Tom makes a fine career in Europe; then at great personal sacrifice, he returns to the American South in order to serve his own people.

Ice Cream From Heaven. (Skinner, Theodosia B.), 1962.

A bright seven-year-old comes to live with her aunt's family in the North after the death of her mother. She is amazed at the sight of indoor bathrooms, white children in classrooms, and snow which she calls ice cream from heaven. As Rebecca Ann grows up, her aunt's family encounters hard times and she bears the brunt of the changes. Still, her attitude is one of gratitude at having escaped the harsher reality of life in the South. Before she marries, Rebecca and her fiancée travel south again to bring her grandmother to live with them in the North.

Iola Leroy, or Shadows Uplifted. (Harper, Frances Ellen Watkins), 1892.

The story depicts plantation life in the final days of the Civil War and the prejudice and injustice encountered by American blacks in the North after the conflict. The tale centers on the sensational experiences of Iola Leroy, a beautiful mulatto who is tricked into slavery by a villainous cousin. Iola proves to be a defiant slave whom none of a series of masters can reduce to concubinage. Rescued by Union soldiers, Iola serves the cause of freedom as a nurse. She is wooed by Dr. Gresham, a Massachusetts aristocrat, who wants her to abandon her newly discovered Negro identity and marry him. Instead, Iola tells Gresham of her resolve to find her family. Through a series of happy coincidences, members of the Leroy family are united, going thence to live in Boston. Although apparently white, Iola and her brother valiantly remain within the ranks of the Negro race, suffering its economic and social disabilities. The novel attempts to rebut charges regarding the moral degradation of mulattoes, especially women, and Afro-Americans. It expresses support of the temperance crusade and the women's movement, for which the author was a prominent spokeswoman.

Jonah's Gourd Vine. (Hurston, Zora Neale), 1934.

An autobiographical tale about black folk in the South that begins with a long section focused on the relationship between Ned and Amy

Crittenden. Embittered by his experience as a former slave, Ned directs most of his wrath toward John, his stepchild, who has always been noticeably different from the other children. When John grows up, he marries a good woman and moves to Eatonville, Florida, an all-Negro town where he receives the "call" to preach. Despite his spiritual mission, John cannot subdue the sexual element of his personality and is relieved when his wife's death frees him of the marriage. His marriage to a slattern three months later costs him the position of State Church Convention Moderator, a post he has held for nine years. Hard times ensue and John marries a third time. Though he begins to preach again, he is overcome once more by sexual passion. Returning home to his wife after an assignation with another woman, John is killed when his car is struck by a train. Despite his sins, John is shown to be an authentic spiritual leader of his people. He is God's true representative, and his struggle to reconcile his holy calling with his human failings is the struggle that all human beings face.

Kenneth. (Wright, Zara), 1920.

Kenneth, a minor character in *Black and White Tangled Threads*, also written by Wright, is the son of Guy Randolph, the man whose wife abandoned him. Guy lives as a white but fulfills his obligation to fellow blacks by using his legal skills in their behalf. Most of the tale concerns Phillip Grayson, a brilliant black doctor whose life and career are threatened by the unwelcome attentions of a wealthy white patient, Alice Blair. Evil Alice eventually becomes a dedicated Red Cross nurse in Europe during the First World War. She and Grayson meet again in a hospital there, and they reconcile. The plot continues interminably, focusing next on the troubles of Kenneth's wife, Diann, who almost loses him to Zoleeta's beautiful daughter Agnes. Alas, Diann discovers that she too is of royal blood. Moreover, she has prior claim to the Blankleigh estate, which she nobly refuses to press.

Killer of the Dream. (Roberson, Sadie L.), 1963.

Three short stories and an epilogue which resolves problems outlined in each tale. In "The Color," a drifter conquers alcoholism and settles down to what he hopes is a steady job. However, a racial incident forces him back on the road. In "The Creed," a Jewish brother and sister compensate for social rejection by frantically acquiring material goods. A world-renowned singer in "The Nationality" complains that the war (World War II) has left her career in ruins and that no one remembers or cares about her heroism in the French underground. The Statue of Liberty tells each of them that hatred and prejudice are killers of the dream of freedom and that each must return to the world and wage a committed battle for freedom.

"Let My People Go." (Wood, Lillian E.), 1921.

An angry, assertive novel that describes the militant, post–World War I mood of black Americans. Bob McComb returns from service abroad and realizes he has been betrayed by his country. The Klan rides again and there is rioting in the streets of northern cities. After graduating from law school, McComb becomes a civil rights investigator in the South. Later, as leader of the Race Equality Party, he advocates race pride, wide-scale political involvement of Afro-Americans, and limited organizational self-segregation. As a congressman, he meets with the president of the United States and presents evidence of racial injustice. He makes an eloquent plea for equal rights. Many followers have suffered and died to see him elected. Like McComb, they have come to believe that their humanity depends on commitment to a political struggle for equal rights.

Like One of the Family. (Childress, Alice), 1956.

A series of conversations (which, in effect are brief fictional essays) between a household worker and her best friend Madge. The two black women discuss Madge's relationships with white female employers in addition to the race question in general, black men and children, the meaning of the war (World War II), etc. Intended as a primer for white people, the story is meant to reveal the human side of the dark women who are employed in their homes.

The Living Is Easy. (West, Dorothy), 1948.

The story of Cleo Judson, a power-mad woman driven to control the lives of others, and black Bostonians, a unique and closed society, described in the novel as "a counterfeit of the Brahmin cult." Through lies and other forms of deceit, Cleo tricks her sisters into leaving their husbands in order to come to live with her. She achieves her other dream of becoming part of Boston's black upper class. In achieving her ends, Cleo ruins the lives of her family and others. Finding her husband useful only for the money he earns, Cleo denies him all warmth, understanding, and sexual companionship. In the end, she is left alone as one by one her family deserts her. Still, Cleo learns nothing and remains selfish and evil. In the final scene, she considers ways she can steal the affection shared by her daughter and the daughter's five-year-old cousin.

The Maddening Scar. (Clinton, Dorothy Randle), 1962.

A mystery tale with a moral. A young college student aspires to sing classical music in spite of a speech impediment. When a professor who has publicly embarrassed Vivian Dale is found dead, Dale becomes the principal suspect. Eventually the actual murderer is found, and in an incredible turn of the plot, Dale is given his big break at professional singing by a contrite promoter whose brother was a talented but unrecognized writer—with poor penmanship analogous to Dale's lisp—who worked himself to death in a cheap hotel room. The novel is the extremely weak first effort by a black woman at writing a murder mystery. The main characters in the tale are white.

Maud Martha. (Brooks, Gwendolyn), 1953.

Written with the indirection and concentrated power of poetry, this novel is a collection of delicate vignettes about the life of a plain and sensitive woman who was overshadowed as a child by a more beautiful sister. Maud Martha marries a poor black man who wishes she had yellow skin. For her part, Maud Martha wishes his manners were less crude and that he loved her more. Her remarkable life is beset by the commonplace afflictions and joys of growing up and living as an ordinary black woman. Nothing in Maud's experience convinces her that life itself is not good. Nothing overpowers her sense of self-worth and dignity—not even her negative encounters with white folk. As World War II draws to a close, Maud becomes pregnant with her second child.

Megda. (Kelly, Emma Dunham), 1891.

A tale of "white" mulattoes whose Christian religion and Victorian conduct are idealized. The problem of the story is the conflict between religious faith and agnosticism. Fiercely independent and intellectually honest, Megda is isolated from her high school friends after their conversion to Christianity. Her chief adversary and the leader of the new group is Ethel Lawton. Because of her lack of faith, Megda loses Reverend Stanley's love to Ethel who, on the eve of their wedding, dies an untimely but peaceful death. Inspired by her rival's calm acceptance of her fate, Megda heeds Ethel's death-bed request that

Megda spread the faith in Ethel's stead. Megda keeps her promise. Four years later she marries Stanley. The story ends with the death of another of Megda's school-girl acquaintances. Unlike the serious and faithful Ethel, Maude, who led a life of irresponsible ease, is left unprepared to meet her Maker. Maude's last moments are filled with abject terror and shameless begging. With Christlike magnanimity, Megda and Stanley promise to care for Maude's little girl and to give the child their name.

Memphis Jackson's Son. (Beechwood, Mary), 1956.

The medical degree earned by a black farm boy from Cotter's Crossing, Virginia, is a personal triumph over humble origins and the vice of gambling. Only with his mother's encouragement and assistance is Ken Jackson able to achieve this victory. The author tries to show that white people in the South, like blacks, are in the process of change. Parallel to Ken's story is that of the Princhetts, owners of Claymore plantation in upper Tidewater Virginia, where the black people of Cotter's Crossing were held as slaves before the Civil War. Lydia Princhett, a divorcée with liberal ideas, is at odds with her beloved, very conservative brother Frank. Both of them honestly love Memphis, Ken's mother, for her kindness, wisdom, and service to their family. Because of her they learn to welcome the idea of her son becoming a doctor. The story graphically depicts the destructive, narcotic effect of gambling on Ken's personality and, in the character of Lydia, the inevitable stress and discontent that is the lot of the thinking woman.

Moses, Man of the Mountain. (Hurston, Zora Neale), 1939.

An often humorous, extended folk-allegory written in Negro dialect and based on the Exodus story. Depicting both the history and current situation of American blacks, the story offers a nationalistic solution to the race problem. Moses' primary task is to teach the Israelites (black Americans) to relinquish their dependency (expressive of a now inappropriate slave mentality) and accept the responsibility for achieving their own freedom. Blacks, like the ancient Jews in the Exodus story, must become a disciplined people and a unified, self-conscious nation willing to make sacrifices for freedom. In Moses' character, Hurston outlines the personal and spiritual qualities the role of black leader requires.

The Narrows. (Petry, Ann), 1953.

Middle- and upper-class people and institutions have hidden, but real and intimate, links to the ghetto. Race prejudice is so powerful and so pervasive that everyone and every social institution can be affected even when the true goals of social or economic manipulation have little or no relationship to race. In this tale of the interracial love affair of Lincoln Williams and Camillo Treadway, it is clear that neither black nor white society will permit their relationship to remain a private affair. Persons in every strata of life in the community are drawn into the web of violence that causes Link's death.

Of One Blood. (Hopkins, Pauline Elizabeth), 1902.

A strange and complicated fairy tale in which themes of race pride and protest become totally submerged in a fantastical plot. Dianthe Lusk, a Fisk Jubilee singer, meets a magnetic physician. Through the forces of mesmerism, Dianthe sees into her past. Seeing her grandmother in a vision, she learns of the grandmother's inadvertent marriage to both of her brothers. In a complicated series of events beginning in the days of slavery, the grandmother's current husband (and brother) is reared as the child of her mother's former owners. A mysterious force carries the three siblings to the Ethiopian capital of Meroe where they see marvels of that ancient black civilization. Not only do the three siblings learn of a glorious African past, but they discover that one brother is actually a king. His true name is Ergamenes, and he will be married to the lovely Queen Candace.

Our Nig. (Wilson, Harriet E.), 1859.

The first novel known to have been written by an African-American in the United States. This poignant story, which combines elements of the sentimental novel and the Afro-American slave narrative, is the autobiographical account of a young mulatto woman and her life as the virtual slave of a family in the North. Wilson refers to herself on the title page as simply "Our Nig," and doesn't list her given name as the author. Her persona in the story is Alfrado Smith, most frequently referred to as Frado. The story begins with an account of the misfortunes experienced by her mother; her mother's marriage to a black man and his subsequent death; her struggle to survive; and her ultimate abandonment of the six-year-old Frado. The major portion of the novel focuses on the mental and physical abuse Frado suffers as the indentured servant of the Belmont family. It closes with a brief recital of Frado's attempts to care for herself and her child, despite her broken health, when she is deserted by her husband and again, later, after his death. Frado asks that her readers take pity on her and help her support herself and her son, who is ill, by purchasing a copy of her book. Her tale is not a one-sided litany of cruelty. The sadism of Mrs. Belmont is ameliorated to some degree by the kindness of other members of the family. And while she is victimized by the family during the time she lives with them, from the age of six until she is eighteen, Frado learns to fight for her dignity and to question the justice of her treatment.

Passing. (Larsen, Nella), 1929.

Two childhood friends, both fair enough to "pass," take different paths in life. Clare Kendry marries a wealthy white man who hates blacks; Irene Redfield marries a doctor and occupies a secure berth in upper-class black society. Irene is embarrassed when her old friend Clare returns home and wishes to be among her own kind again. A short time later she is stunned to discover that her husband Brian and Clare are having an affair. Despite her anguish, Irene determines that she will not divorce Brian, and she succeeds at pretending not to know of the affair. The experience teaches Irene that she values her social position more than her pride or her husband's love. The story ends ambiguously when Irene attends a party and accidentally (?) pushes Clare through a window to her death.

Plum Bun. (Fauset, Jessie Redmond), 1927.

Junius and Mattie Murray have a light-hearted attitude about the great difference in the color of their skin, but their fair-skinned daughter Angela is struck with the differing treatment, based on color, each of her parents is likely to receive. Determined to possess the best things in life, the "plums" denied to dark-skinned Negroes, Angela goes to New York to "pass." The marriage she hopes for fails to materialize, and she finds herself penniless and involved in a sordid affair with her wealthy white suitor. Meanwhile, her sister Virginia enters the best social circles and becomes engaged to a kind young man. The tale ends happily as the sisters reconcile and Angela returns to the race. The importance of skin color in America almost destroys her life.

Publicans and Sinners. (Shores, Minnie T.), 1960.

A melodrama in which young adults in a Missouri city face numerous complications: some very plausible like those brought on by the war and by racial discrimination and others highly unlikely and which stem from the heroine's capricious personality.

Queen of Persia, the Story of Esther Who Saved Her People. (Cotton, Ella Earls), 1960.

The biblical tale of Esther is shown to contain lessons applicable to the racial situation in America. Vashti, the beloved wife of King Ahasuerus, is driven from the palace and buried alive for refusing to appear nude at a banquet when summoned to do so by the drunken king. Esther, a Jewess, becomes queen; and Haman, the king's chief councilman, convinces King Ahasuerus to kill all the Jews because they are considered to be an unassimilable population in the kingdom. Judaism is in conflict with the kingdom's polytheism and, thus, Jews are a hindrance to its nationalistic goals. To save the Jews, Esther bravely risks her life. She comes into the presence of Ahasuerus without permission and pleads their cause, an act punishable by death. The Jews are saved because of Esther's courage, and Haman and all his family are killed. Cotton maintains that the world has changed little since biblical times. Like Esther and Mordecai, African Americans must remain loyal to their race; each must acknowledge the fact that his fate is tied to that of his fellows.

Quicksand. (Larsen, Nella), 1928.

Helga Crane, daughter of a Danish mother and a black American father, is defeated in her attempt to find a simple kind of happiness in life. She is stifled, in turn, by the atmosphere of a Southern black college; by the intense race-consciousness of a circle of bright, young black New Yorkers; and later, by her categorical acceptance as an "exotic" by her mother's relatives in Sweden. In Sweden, Helga learns that it is not her blackness she hates, but the American racial situation. Shortly after her return to America, she seduces and hurriedly marries a fundamentalist Southern preacher. Back in the South once again, she realizes that the peace she expects to find in unreflecting religion and sexual submission cannot withstand the fact of her actual lack of faith and feelings of deepening revulsion. With horrible clarity, she realizes that she is engulfed by an alien folk culture, by too many children birthed in too rapid succession, and by marriage to a man who repulses her.

The Reign of Terror. (Brown, Mattye Jeanette), 1962.

A rambling, repetitive tale of a black family living in an atmosphere of violence in a Southern community after the Civil War. Knick

Jones becomes the latest target of white terrorism in Wickerville because of the land and property he has acquired and because of his audacious plan to send two of his children to college. Sarah insists that her husband flee when "The Caucus" arrives to question him at midnight. In a powerful scene, she faces the mob with a shotgun, giving Knick a chance to escape and, ultimately, saving herself and the children as well.

The Resentment. (Spencer, Mary Etta), 1921.

The rags-to-riches story of a young boy who becomes "Hog King" of his state. The disrespect and name calling that Silas Miller endures while working for a white farmer are goads to his achievement. On the path to success, Silas clings to his belief in the importance of obtaining an education, avoiding the temptations of city life, and keeping faith in God. Once he succeeds, he shares his wealth with fellow Afro-Americans and engages in the work of racial uplift. The story advocates business enterprise as a means of racial elevation. It charges those who succeed with their moral responsibility to assist their less fortunate brethren.

Scandal at Daybreak. (Wallace, Elizabeth West), 1954.

A beautiful woman from New Orleans seizes the opportunity of World War II to escape with her children from West Bottoms, the Spring City slums, and to move to Quality Hill. Although she works desperately hard, Helene finds she must accept financial assistance, proffered in exchange for companionship and sex, from financially secure men in the black community. After years of struggle, Helene becomes involved in a scandal that can destroy her hope of being accepted by those who live "on the hill." Miraculously, the lawyer who is handling her divorce discovers he loves her and asks her to marry him. In her drive for a better life, Helene discovers the greatest obstacles confronting her are those presented by the snobbery of the black middle class.

Seraph on the Suwanee. (Hurston, Zora Neale), 1948.

A story of love, marriage, and personal growth set in the small lumbering, turpentine-producing towns of Citrabell and Sawley, Florida, in the early years of the twentieth century. Jim Meserve, whose forebears were wealthy planters before the war, comes to Sawley to make his fortune and conquers the town's most recalcitrant and hysterical virgin. The problem with Jim and Arvay's relationship is Arvay's inability, because of timidity and feelings of inferiority, to love Jim with honesty and courage. Jim, an aggressive, resourceful man, finally demands that Arvay face and overcome her feelings and that she become a better person than the prejudiced, narrow-minded, truth-evading coward she has been. It takes more than twenty years of marriage for Arvay to accept her poor white background. She eventually learns to be an honest woman and a worthy mate to the man who has spent years trying to win her mature love. The tale can be read as a call for the attitudes of the old South to be replaced by the best of the new. The Jim Meserves of the South are destined to conquer, and the sooner the Arvays of the world realize it, the happier everyone will be.

She Knew No Evil. (Arnold, Ethel Nishua), 1953.

A story which reveals the writer's keen prejudice against outsiders. Although characters in the story are black, this fact has no bearing on the plot. The leading bachelor in a small town, a young doctor, disappoints everyone by marrying a beautiful outsider from the big city. Just as everyone suspects, the woman proves to be a cold wife and an unloving mother. Moreover, it is eventually discovered that Kimber Winston is actually Singa Ross, a former "numbers" queen and a fugitive from justice. Driven from her home by Winston and his sister, Kimber is killed that very night when her car strikes a tree. Thus, Winston is free to marry Susan, a virtuous, clean-living, hometown girl.

Strange Sinner. (Jordan, Elsie), 1954.

The strange personality of a beautiful, light-skinned woman is the subject of this curious tale. Joan Brooks Blake tries to poison her husband in order to continue an affair with his brother. Just before her husband goes to trial for the murder of another of her lovers whom he has killed accidentally, Joan deserts him. The story attempts to recount the fortunes of two black families after they immigrate to the north. The Blake and Brooks families are connected by the marriage of Joan Brooks and Larry Blake. The tale wanders from a study of the evil mulatto theme to sketchy presentations of the lives of black families who came north from the South around the turn of the century.

The Street. (Petry, Ann), 1946; 1961.

A powerful, naturalistic novel in which the ghetto inexorably claims as victims a young mother and her eight-year-old son. Lutie Johnson's plan to secure a suitable home for herself and her son Bub are doomed from the start. While working away from home as a live-in domestic for a Connecticut family, Lutie loses her husband to another woman. From this white family, she absorbs a belief in the possibilities for economic success in America. This faith sustains her through four years of night school and employment in a steam laundry until she gains employment as a file clerk. Determined to fight the street for Bub's sake, Lutie accepts a singing job in a night club, only to have it snatched from her grasp at the last moment. As time passes, she becomes more worried and enraged. At the breaking point, she bludgeons Boots Smith to death when it becomes clear that he intends to rape her and leave her to Junto, a mysterious white man who wants her to be his mistress. Believing Bub will be better off without a murderess for a mother, Lutie boards a train for Chicago abandoning her son to his fate on the New York City streets.

Their Eyes Were Watching God. (Hurston, Zora Neale), 1937; 1969.

A well-made novel that centers on the personal development of Janie Starks, her growth from girlhood to womanhood as affected by her relationships with three men. Just as Janie enters puberty, her grandmother, out of love and fear for Janie's future, forces her to marry an aging landowner and respected member of the black community. When she runs away from Killicks with a stranger named Joe Starks, Janie's life enters a new phase. As the years pass, Jody (who eventually becomes mayor in the all-Negro town of Eatonville, Florida and its wealthiest citizen) becomes increasingly abusive, demanding that Janie be modest and subservient toward him but remote and superior before the townsfolk. Janie is forced to hide the existence of her inner self and knows only relief when Jody finally dies. In the last act, a gay, irrepressible man, thirteen years her junior, enters Janie's quiet widowhood and teaches her the meaning of love and equal partnership. Yet, in the end, Janie learns that neither economic security, respectability, nor love itself are worth the sacrifices of self that women make for them.

There Is Confusion. (Fauset, Jessie Redmond), 1924.

Middle-class black Philadelphians lead exemplary lives that demonstrate the absurdity of race prejudice. World War I is the catalyst that modifies and clarifies the values of the leading characters. Philip Marshall, who is driven by a desire to serve the race, finally marries a girl of the poorer class. Peter Bye relinquishes his financial dependence on white relatives and also his hatred of them. Joanna achieves the worldly success she craves and settles down to married life. The dominant concern in the story is the confusion caused by race prejudice which is made to seem the more irrational by these revelations of the commonplace hopes and dreams of middle-class Afro-Americans.

Tragedies of Life. (Pitts, Gertrude), 1939.

A short, melodramatic tale of wicked and ungrateful children born in the third generation after freedom. The story opens in 1870. Ignorant and illiterate, Uncle Sam and Aunt Sue do not know that legalized slavery has ended. Despite their late start at freedom, however, the impoverished couple provide their children with a good education and more than an adequate start in life. While their children take advantage of all the opportunities presented to them, the children of the next generation are thoroughly spoiled and sinful. Caring nothing for the sacrifices of their parents and forbears, they are cruelly punished. A son dies in the electric chair and a daughter, after helping her boyfriend rob and kill her mother, is murdered by the boyfriend, who dismembers and burns her body. The story illustrates the loss of moral fiber in the current generation of middle-class black American children; it admonishes parents to return to the old-fashioned principles of religious and moral training.

Under the Cottonwood. (Graham, Katheryn Campbell), 1941.

An autobiographical family chronical set in Penhook, Texas. The tale, spanning the years between the Civil War and the Great Depression, contains a long section devoted to the reminiscences of seventeen old men, former slaves, whose tales of the early days of freedom fascinated Graham as a child. In the story of Mamie's growing up, Graham also records the longstanding ties of loyalty and affection that bind the black and white branches of the Stearns family. The story ends as Mamie, a college-educated woman who is married to an insurance executive, returns to Penhook (Paris, Texas) with her husband and daughter. Most of the old men are dead, and the cottonwood tree, under which she listened to tales of freedom when she was a young girl, is burned to the ground.

Vengeance Is Mine. (Vaught, Estella V.), 1959.

A convoluted tale about the ill-starred life of a young girl (possibly insane) born with six fingers on each hand. Cleo's grievances against the world are many. When her father returns from the Second World War, a wealthy banker refuses to lend him money. Later, her brother is killed by a relative of the very same banker. Very soon after the untimely death of her modest, retiring mother, her father marries a flagrantly sensual widow. Out of revenge for all these painful occurrences, Cleo jilts the nephew of the banker. She deliberately breaks a valued heirloom belonging to the widow. In another town, she changes her name and tricks the son of a wealthy family into marrying her. Numerous turns of the plot find her on her deathbed, repenting of her career of vengeance. Along the way, she gives up her prejudices against Jews, black Americans, and Indians.

A View From the Hill. (Forte, Christine [Christine Forster], 1964.

The simple story of Josie Hamilton, a modest woman who accepts herself and her limitations along with the misfortunes life brings her. Josie survives the deaths of her parents, the loss of her husband in the Second World War, the disgrace brought to the family by a daughter who bears an illegitimate child and leaves the child with Josie to rear. Because of Josie's understanding, the child makes a good life despite having been ostracized as a girl. The child, now a grown woman, returns to Parson's Village after an absence of many years and realizes that her bitter memories of the town are gone and only her love for Josie remains.

Wasted Travail. (Rosebrough, Sadie Mae), 1951.

A sad story written in tortuous language about the pain of a young woman's life. Ostensibly a fictional account, the tale is a first-person interior monologue that appears to be a veiled autobiography. A young black woman, unloved by her work-deadened mother, lives on a farm in the South. She drives a bus to make ends meet and later works in a munitions plant. Eventually she marries and attends college but is beset with frequent illness. In the midst of her pain, she finds solace in the platitudinous talk of her well-meaning white physician. Still, she ultimately resolves her emotional conflicts negatively through complete self-abnegation. She believes that the American racial situation is just. Therefore, when neighbors march in protest of the shooting death of a young man who is caught trying to steal a car, she is ashamed not only of the thief but also of the marchers. The wasted travail of the title refers to the labor pains endured by her mother at the young woman's birth.

Wolf Kitty. (Bellinger, Claudia), 1958.

A childless black couple take in orphans and teach them to avoid evil (especially gambling) and to adhere to Christian principles. These child-rearing practices of Mary Jane Brooks, who is Sammy Marshall's foster mother, are favorably compared to the harsh, unloving methods of Ella Blackman, grandmother of three of Sammy's playmates, who works from dawn to dusk to support herself and the children left in her care.

Yulan. (Washington, Doris V.), 1964.

An embassy secretary witnesses political intrigue and bloodshed as Yulan (an imaginary country on the west coast of Africa) approaches a presidential election—an election that is a travesty of the democratic process. In an orgy of violence, young radicals who had hoped to democratize the government are cruelly murdered by the president's principal advisor. President Parker, who wants to retain his dictatorial power while only pretending to head a democratic state, has greatly improved living conditions in Yulan. The writer, whose persona in the story is the secretary, Audrey, actually worked for the U.S. State Department in Africa. She was obviously struck by the sight of blacks at the seat of power and by the complexity of an African society which, while it does not have a race problem like that in the United States, is free of neither class conflict nor politically motivated cruelty.

BIBLIOGRAPHY OF
SECONDARY SOURCES

Books

Abraham, W. E. *The Mind of Africa*. Chicago: University of Chicago Press, Phoenix Books, 1962.

American Society of African Culture. *The American Negro Writer and His Roots*. Selected Papers from the First Conference of Negro Writers, March 1959. New York: The American Society of African Culture, 1960.

Baker, Houston, Jr. *Black Literature in America*. New York: McGraw-Hill, 1971.

Barkesdale, Richard, and Kinnamon, Kenneth. *Black Writers of America*. New York: Macmillan, 1972.

Barton, Rebecca Chalmers. *Black Voices in American Fiction, 1900–1930*. Oakdale, N.Y.: Dowling College Press, 1976.

———. *Race Consciousness and the American Negro: A Study of the Correlation Between the Group Experience and the Fiction of 1900–1939*. Copenhagen: A. Busck, 1934.

Bigsby, C.W.E. *The Second Black Renaissance*. Westport, Conn.: Greenwood Publishing Co., 1980.

Bone, Robert. *The Negro Novel in America*. New Haven, Conn.: Yale University Press, 1965.

Bontemps, Arna, ed. *The Harlem Renaissance Remembered*. New York: Dodd, Mead, 1972.

Brawley, Benjamin G. *The Negro in Literature and Art*. New York: Duffield, 1929.

Broderick, Francis L., and Meier, August, eds. *Negro Protest Thought in the Twentieth Century*. New York: Bobbs-Merrill, 1965.

Brotz, Howard, ed. *Negro Social and Political Thought*. New York: Basic Books, 1966.

Bruck, Peter, and Karrer, Wolfgang. *The Afro-American Novel Since 1960*. Amsterdam: B. R. Gruner Publishing Co., 1982.

Butterfield, Stephen. *Black Autobiography in America*. Amherst: University of Massachusetts Press, 1974.

Cayton, Horace R. "Ideological Forces in the Work of Negro Writers." In *Anger and Beyond*, pp. 37–50. Edited by Herbert Hill. New York: Harper & Row, 1966.

Christian, Barbara. *Black Women Novelists*. Westport, Conn.: Greenwood Publishing Co., 1980.

Du Bois, W.E.B., and Washington, Booker T. *The Negro in the South: His Economic Progress in Relation to His Moral and Religious Development*. William Levi Bull Lectures. Philadelphia: G.W. Jacobs, 1907; reprint ed., AMS Press, 1973.

Ellison, Ralph W. *Shadow and Act*. New York: The New American Library, A Signet Book, 1966.

Factor, Robert L. *The Black Response to America*. Reading, Mass.: Addison-Wesley, 1970.

Ford, Nick A. *The Contemporary Negro Novel*. Boston: Meador Publishing Co.; reprint ed., College Park, Md.: McGrath Publishing Co., 1968.

Franklin, John Hope. *From Slavery to Freedom*. New York: Random House, Vintage Books, 1969.

Frazier, E. Franklin. "La Bourgeoisie Noire." In *Anthology of American Negro Literature*. Edited by Victor F. Calverton. New York: The Modern Library, 1929.

Frazier, E. Franklin. *The Negro in the United States*. New York: Macmillan, 1949.

Fredrickson, George H. *The Black Image in the White Mind; The Debate on Afro-American Character and Destiny, 1817–1914*. New York: Harper & Row, 1971.

Gates, Henry Louis, Jr. Introduction and notes to *Our Nig; or, Sketches from the Life of a Free Black*, by Harriet A. Wilson. New York: Random House, 1983.

Gloster, Hugh M. *Negro Voices in American Fiction*. Chapel Hill: University of North Carolina Press, 1948.

Harley, Sharon, and Terborg-Penn, Rosalyn, eds. *The Afro-American*

Woman: Struggles and Images. Port Washington, N.Y.: National University Publications, Kennikat Press, 1978.

Hemenway, Robert. "Hurston's Buzzards and Elijah's Ravens." In *A Rainbow Round Her Shoulder: The Zora Neale Hurston Symposium Papers.* Edited by Ruthe T. Sheffey. Baltimore, Md.: Morgan State University Press, 1982.

Hoffman, Frederick J. *The Modern Novel in America.* Revised edition. Chicago: Henry Regnery Co., 1963.

Howard, Lillie P. *Zora Neale Hurston.* Boston: Twayne Publishers, A Division of G. K. Hall & Co., 1980.

Huggins, Nathan I.; Kilson, Martin; and Fox, Daniel M. *Key Issues in the Afro-American Experience.* New York: Harcourt Brace Jovanovich, 1971.

Hughes, John Milton Charles [Carl Milton Hughes]. *The Negro Novelist.* New York: Citadel Press, 1953.

Hull, Gloria T.; Scott, Patricia Bell; and Smith, Barbara, eds. *But Some of Us Are Brave.* Old Westbury, N.Y.: The Feminist Press, 1982.

Hurston, Zora Neale. *Dust Tracks on a Road.* Introduction by Darwin Turner. New York: J. B. Lippincott, 1942.

Lee, Robert A., ed. *Black Fiction: New Studies in the Afro-American Novel Since 1945.* London: Vision Press, 1980.

Lerner, Gerda, ed. *Black Women in White America.* New York: Patheon Books, 1972.

Levine, Lawrence W. *Black Culture and Black Consciousness; Afro-American Folk Thought from Slavery to Freedom.* New York: Oxford University Press, 1977.

Littlejohn, David. *Black on White.* New York: Viking Press, 1966.

Locke, Alain, ed. *The New Negro.* 1925. In *Studies in American Life.* Edited by August Meier, reprint ed. New York: Atheneum, 1970.

Logan, Rayford W. *The Negro in American Life and Thought.* New York: Macmillan, Collier Books, 1970.

Loggins, Vernon. *The Negro Author: His Development in America.* New York: Columbia University Press, 1931.

Meier, August. "Negro Class Structure and Ideology in the Age of Booker T. Washington." In *America's Black Past*, pp. 266–75. Edited By Eric Foner. New York: Harper & Row, 1970.

———. *Negro Thought in America, 1880–1915.* Ann Arbor: University of Michigan Press, Ann Arbor Paperbacks, 1970.

Meier, August, and Rudwick, Elliott, eds. *The Making of Black America*, vols. I and II. In *Studies in American Life.* Edited by August Meier. New York: Atheneum, 1969.

Miller, Kelly. *Out of the House of Bondage*. New York: Neale Publishing Co., 1914; reprint ed. New York: Schocken Books, 1971.

Mossell, N.F. *The Work of Afro-American Women*. Freeport, N.Y.: Books for Libraries Press, 1971.

Quarles, Benjamin. *Black Abolitionists*. New York: Oxford University Press, 1969.

———. *The Negro in the Making of America*. New York: Collier Books, 1969.

Rosenblatt, Roger. *Black Fiction*. Cambridge: Harvard University Press, 1974.

Singh, Amritjit. *The Novels of the Harlem Renaissance*. University Park, Pa.: Pennsylvania State University Press, 1976.

Smith, Sidonie. *Where I'm Bound*. Westport, Conn.: Greenwood Publishing Co., 1974.

Stuckey, Sterling. *The Ideological Origins of Black Nationalism*. Boston: Beacon Press, 1972.

Tate, Claudia, ed. *Black Women Writers at Work*. New York: Continuum Publishing Co., 1983.

Thorpe, Earl E. *The Central Theme of Black History*. Durham, N.C.: Seeman Printing, 1969.

———. *The Mind of the Negro: An Intellectual History of the Afro-American*. Baton Rouge, La.: Ortlieb Press, 1961.

Toomer, Jean. *Cane*. New York: Boni & Liveright, 1923; Harper & Row, 1969.

Whitlow, Roger. *Black American Literature: A Critical History*. Chicago: Nelson Hall, 1973.

Williams, John A., and Harris, Charles F., eds. *Amistad 1*. New York: Random House, Vintage Books, 1970.

———. *Amistad 2*. New York: Random House, Vintage Books, 1971.

Williams, Kenny J. *They Also Spoke: An Essay on Negro Literature in America, 1787–1930*. Nashville, Tenn.: Townsend, 1970.

Young, James O. *Black Writers of the Thirties*. Baton Rouge: Louisiana State University Press, 1973.

Articles

Abramowitz, Jack. "Crossroads of Negro Thought, 1890–1895." *Social Education* 18 (March 1954):117–20.

Bell, Howard H. "National Negro Conventions of the Middle 1840s:

Moral Suasion vs Political Action." *The Journal of Negro History* 42 (October 1957):247–60.

Bellow, Saul. "Recent American Fiction." *American Studies International* 15 (Spring 1977):7–18.

Bland, Edward. "Racial Bias and Negro Poetry." *Poetry* 43 (March 1944):328–29.

———. "Social Forces Shaping the Negro Novel." *Negro Quarterly*, Fall 1942, pp. 241–48.

Braithwaite, William S. "The Novels of Jessie Fauset." *Opportunity* 12 (January 1934):24–28.

Brawley, Benjamin. "The Negro Literary Renaissance." *Southern Workman* 56 (April 1927):177–84.

Brown, Lloyd. "Which Way for the Negro Writer?" *Masses and Mainstream* 4 (March 1951):53–63; (April 1951):50–59.

Brown, Sterling. "Our Literary Audience." *Opportunity* 8 (February 1930):42–46, 61.

Bullock, Penelope. "The Mulatto in American Fiction." *Phylon* 6 (First Quarter 1945):78–82.

Burgum, Edwin Berry. "Review of *The Chinaberry Tree* by Jessie Fauset." *Opportunity* 10 (March 1932):88.

Byrd, James W. "Zora Neale Hurston: A Novel Folklorist." *Tennessee Folklore Society Bulletin* 21 (June 1955):37–41.

Chapman, Abraham. "The Harlem Renaissance in Literary History." *College Language Association Journal* 11 (November 1961):38–58.

Chestnut, Charles. "Post–Bellum, Pre–Harlem." *Crisis* 38 (June 1931):193–94.

Davis, Allison. "Our Negro Intellectuals." *Crisis* 35 (August 1928):268–84, 286.

Daykin, Walter L. "Social Thought in Negro Novels." *Sociology and Social Research* 29 (January-February 1935):247–52.

Dempsey, David. "Uncle Tom's Ghost and the Literary Abolitionist." *Antioch Review* 6 (September 1946):442–48.

Du Bois, W.E.B. Editorial. *The Crisis* 1 (November 1910):10.

Du Bois, W.E.B., and Locke, Alain. "The Younger Literary Movement." *The Crisis* 27 (November 1927):161–63.

Ellison, Ralph. "Recent Negro Fiction." *New Masses*, August 1951, pp. 22–26.

Ford, Nick Aaron. "The Negro Novel as a Vehicle of Propaganda." *Quarterly Review of Higher Education Among Negroes* 9 (July 1941):135–39.

Frazier, E. Franklin. "The Garvey Movement." *Opportunity* 4 (November 1926):346–48.

———. "The Negro's New Leaders." *Current History* 28 (April 1928):56–59.

Glicksberg, Charles I. "The Alienation of Negro Literature." *Phylon* 9 (First Quarter 1950):49–58.

———. "The Negro Cult of the Primitive." *Antioch Review* 4 (March 1944): 47–55.

Hopkins, Pauline. "Munroe Rogers." *The Colored American Magazine*, November 6, 1902, pp. 21–23.

Hughes, Langston. "The Negro Artist and the Racial Mountain." *Nation*, January 1926, pp. 692–94.

Johnson, James W. "The Dilemma of the Negro Author." *American Mercury*, December 1928, pp. 447–81.

———. "Race Prejudice and the Negro Artist." *Harpers*, November 1928, pp. 769–76.

Keith, Allyn. "A Note on Negro Nationalism." *New Challenge* (Fall 1937):65–69.

Lash, John S. "The Race Consciousness of the American Negro Author." *Social Forces* 28 (October 1949):24–34.

Lee, Ulysses. "Criticism at Mid-Century." *Phylon* 9 (Fourth Quarter, 1950):328–37.

Locke, Alain. "American Literary Tradition and the Negro." *The Modern Quarterly* 3 (May-July 1926):215–22.

Neal, Larry. "The Black Arts Movement." *The Drama Review* 12 (Summer 1968):29–39.

Park, Robert. "Negro Race Consciousness as Reflected in Race Literature." *American Review* 1 (September-October 1923):505–17.

Redding, Jay Saunders. "American Negro Literature." *American Scholar* 18 (Spring 1949): 137–48.

Starkey, Marion L. "Jessie Fauset." *Southern Workman* 61 (May 1932):217–20.

Thurman, Wallace. "Negro Artists and the Negro." *New Republic*, August 31, 1927, pp. 37–39.

Updike, John. "The Cultural Situation of the American Writer." *American Studies International* 15 (Spring 1977):19–28.

Walker, Robert H. "Patterns in Recent American Literature." *Stetson University Bulletin* 65 (October 1967):1–12.

Wright, Richard. "I Bite the Hands That Feed Me." *Atlantic Monthly*, June 1940, pp. 826–28.

Other Sources

Bunche, Ralph. "Conceptions and Ideologies of the Negro Program." Memoranda for the Carnegie-Gunnar Myrdal Study of the Negro in America, 1940.
————. "Programs, Ideologies, Tactics and Achievements of Negro Betterment and Interracial Organizations." Memoranda for the Carnegie-Gunnar Myrdal Study of the Negro in America, 1940.
Jackson, Augusta V. "The Renascence of Negro Literature 1922 to 1929." Master's thesis, Atlanta University, 1936.
Jackson, George Blyden. "Of Irony in Negro Fiction: A Critical Study." Ph.D. dissertation, University of Michigan, 1953.

INDEX

n.42, 138-39; and education in *Iola Leroy,* 14-19, 30 n.19; and education in *"Let My People Go,"* 35-36, 44-45; and novels by black American women as examples of, 9, 72; in *The Resentment,* 35-36; and Self-help, 43-45; and the temperance crusade, 18-19, 30 n.30; and views of Booker T. Washington, 21; and W.E.B. Du Bois, 12, 21

Vaught, Estella V., *Vengeance Is Mine,* 151
Vengeance Is Mine (Vaught), 151
A View From the Hill (Forte [Christine Forster]), 88, 93-94, 98 n.4, 99 n.7, 151
Vroman, Mary E., *Esther,* 137

Wallace, Elizabeth West, *Scandal at Daybreak,* 147
Wamble, Thelma, *All in the Family,* 132
Washington, Booker T., 21, 65 n.42; and economic national-

ism, 62 n.29; as fictional character in *Contending Forces,* 25-26
Washington, Doris V., *Yulan,* 152
Wasted Travail (Rosebrough), 98 n.4, 151-52
West, Dorothy, *The Living Is Easy,* 141-42
Wilson, Harriet E., *Our Nig,* 144-45
Wolf Kitty (Bellinger), 98 n.4, 152
Women, black American: concept of beauty of, in novels by black women, 66 n.52; in *The Flaming Sword,* 66 n.53; as theme in novels by black American women, 8, 61 n.1, 72-73, 81, 98 n.5
Wood, Lillian E., *"Let My People Go,"* 141
Wood, Odella Phelps, *High Ground,* 138
Wright, Richard, 56, 107
Wright, Zara: *Black and White Tangled Threads,* 133-34; *Kenneth,* 140

Yulan (Washington), 152

About the Author

CAROLE McALPINE WATSON is an administrator at the National Endowment for the Humanities. She has been a consultant to the U.S. Department of Education, Director of Inter-Cultural Programs at the Lindenwood Colleges in Saint Charles, Missouri, and founding faculty member and chair of the English Department at Opportunity School in Saint Louis, Missouri.